How To Build
A Hot Tuner Car

How To Build
A Hot Tuner Car

Scott "Sky" Smith

MOTORBOOKS

First published in 2007 by Motorbooks, an imprint of MBI Publishing Company LLC, Galtier Plaza, Suite 200, 380 Jackson Street, St. Paul, MN 55101 USA

Motorbooks titles are also available at discounts in bulk quantity for industrial or sales-promotional use. For details write to Special Sales Manager at MBI Publishing Company, Galtier Plaza, Suite 200, 380 Jackson Street, St. Paul, MN 55101 USA.

To find out more about our books, join us online at www.motorbooks.com.

Library of Congress Cataloging-in-Publication Data

Smith, Scott, 1958 Aug. 18-
   How to build a hot tuner car / by Scott Sky Smith.
      p. cm.
   ISBN-13: 978-0-7603-2912-2 (softbound)
   ISBN-10: 0-7603-2912-5 (softbound)
   1. Hot rods. 2. Automobiles, Foreign—Performance. I. Title.
TL236.3.S655 2007
629.28'786--dc22

                              2007012455

Editor: Jennifer Bennett

Printed in China

On the cover:
Main: This is one hot Honda with doors from LSD. *Courtesy Lambo Style Doors*

Inset: Using a short ram air intake not only improves engine performance, but it really cleans up the engine compartment.

On the title page: Lambo-style doors will make any vehicle look like an upper-end car—even a Honda Civic. The best part is that they are affordable and easy to install.

On the back cover: As the author applies the graphics, he removes the clear outer sheet, pulling it at a 180-degree angle from the vehicle.

CONTENTS

ABOUT THE AUTHOR

Scott "Sky" Smith grew up in a family-owned business that included rebuilding wrecked cars, fiberglass manufacturing, and metal fabrication. He has a Bachelor of Science degree in Industrial Arts from Iowa State University and taught auto mechanics at the high school level. His first custom car was a Meyers Towd and he has had numerous vehicles since then, including a Triumph TR6, Corvettes, Mustangs, RX7s, Porsches, and more. Mr. Smith has been educating consumers as a columnist and a public speaker for years and is the author of *How to Buy a Single-Engine Airplane* and *Ultimate Boat Maintenance Project,* published by Motorbooks. His work has appeared in numerous publications, including the *Ankeny Press Citizen, Welcome Home Magazine, The Des Moines Register, Private Pilot, Custom Planes, Cessna Owners Magazine, Piper Owners Magazine, US Aviator, Sport Aerobatics, Dockside, Yacht Trader,* and *Aero Trader.*

ACKNOWLEDGMENTS

I have said it before and I will say it again, it takes more than one person to write a book. In my case it is my wife and business and life partner, Jeanne, who keeps me going and helps me get everything organized and put together. She also helps me stay on task. Jeanne is an accomplished writer, business executive, and motivator—Jeanne is an invaluable asset. I would be remiss if I didn't thank my kids, Zach and Aerielle. In fact, if it weren't for Aerielle's desire for a new car I might not have tackled a tuner car as a project. It's also important to thank them for their assistance in the photo shoots, and for helping at home and at the office so I had the free time needed for writing.

As a custom-car, aviation, and marine insurance agency owner, I have to acknowledge the assistance of my staff in helping me complete this book. Without them running the day-to-day operations of the business, I wouldn't have been able to spend the extra time necessary writing and gathering the information and photos.

Thanks definitely go to Josh Knichel for his help and connections in the tuner industry. His experience in the tuner car market was critical in our decisions for the modifications. Knichel, Performance Import Trends, and Dee Zee Manufacturing provided support, time, and the use of his contacts and experience. And I can't forget all the manufacturers that helped. We used KW Automotive North America (which distributes the LSD vertical doors and the ST Suspensions Speed Tech Springs), Razzi Ground Effects, Nitrous Express, Auto Meter Products, Inc., Sharpline Graphics, Superior Dash Panels, and The Tire Rack.

It was also very difficult to take pictures and work on the car at the same time, so it is important to mention Scott Hendricks and Eric Stall, two very good friends who helped do the work. Without both, I wouldn't have gotten the modifications completed.

Even though this book is about owner modifications, I did talk to others, and any comments gleaned from talking to manufacturers and mechanics is a great reminder of why some things are better left to the professionals.

Numerous other manufacturers, dealers, and owners have provided information, products, and advice for the book. Big thanks go out to all of them for their enthusiasm and assistance to help tuner car owners learn a little more about their cars and make the affordable projects go a little easier. Hopefully I didn't forget any of you!

CHAPTER 1
TOOLS, EQUIPMENT AND SAFETY TIPS

With this book I wanted to show people that they don't need a really fancy workshop to do modifications. I don't have a $100,000 workshop and I don't have a car lift, but what I do have is a nice garage with room to do my work, the tools necessary to complete the work, and a few contacts who have more equipment than I do.

Even though I don't have a huge, expensive shop, I do want a well-equipped shop. Who doesn't? I've never been one to borrow or rent my tools. I like to own. If possible, though, instead of investing in new tools right away, take a look at the cost and the frequency of use of a tool compared to the cost of having a mechanic do the service. This is some-

thing that's especially important with installing any special parts or making any unique modifications. If the project you are undertaking requires a tool or piece of equipment that is a one-of-a-kind or one-time use, why buy?

In this case, the only thing I needed to rent was a spring compressor from the local O'Reilly Auto Parts. Without it I would have had difficulty removing the strut springs. O'Reilly is one of many auto parts stores that offer tools on a loan or rental basis. It might seem like a better idea to buy if the rental price is too high, and that might be the case in some locations, but wasn't in mine. In the end you really have to decide how often you will use the tools before you

The only tool I borrowed was a spring compressor. Without it, I would not have been able to compress the springs on the front strut or rear shocks to remove them. Trying to remove the springs without compressing is extremely dangerous.

Having a large toolbox is not a requirement, but keeping your tools clean, organized, and accessible will make the projects go faster. I bought this Craftsman roller box on sale.

make that decision. I have to be honest here; I do have tools in my shop that I have only used once. But that is because I couldn't borrow or rent the item.

Also, sometimes it is better to have a professional shop do the job than to spend the money on one tool. In my case, that was when the Razzi ground effects package was fitted and ready for paint. My garage was not warm enough, or dirt-free enough, to give the parts the paint job I wanted. I talked to a local body shop and made arrangements to drop off the parts fitted and ready for installation. After paint, I picked up the parts, took them home, and installed them. They were dirt-free and gorgeous. Okay, it wasn't an owner-painted part, but it sure took the pressure off me to get the shop clean.

Make sure you have a copy of the car's owner's manual and a service and parts manual. Service and parts manuals will save you time figuring out how to access and remove items. It's amazing how fast a job goes when you have the correct information and tools. Manuals will be vital resources of information for your car.

WARRANTIES

The manufacturers don't usually recommend the modifications we will talk about in the book, and the projects will probably void your warranty if your car is covered under one. If your car is a newer model and still under warranty, make sure that you understand that the warranty will be void once you start adding things such as nitrous, vertical doors, and new exhaust systems. Also, don't think that modifying your car means you don't need to service the other items like batteries, antifreeze, or even oil changes. Adding nitrous, headers, and other components can actually put more stress on your engine, requiring additional maintenance.

TOOLS

Any basic toolbox should be equipped with enough tools to complete most of the projects in this book. Average owners don't need the top-of-the-line tool or every imaginable tool designed. What they do need is a good selection of quality tools. A prepackaged set is a pretty good way to buy tools, and while different cars might require different tools, you can't go wrong if you have an assorted set of screwdrivers, nut drivers (or a nut-driver handle and assorted small sockets), pliers, long-nose pliers, diagonal cutters, sharp knife, wire strippers, an adjustable wrench, socket set, extensions, and ratchets. Make sure that you buy the standard and metric sockets and include a spark plug socket. It's always good to buy a set of standard and metric combination wrenches (the ratcheting kind are nice but not necessary), and a small (maybe big) hammer. Kits with these

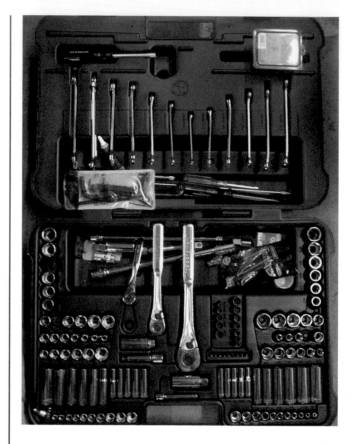

You can purchase complete tool kits at reasonable prices. This tool kit contains metric and standard sockets, ratchets (in ¼-, ⅜-, and ½-inch drives), and a few assorted wrenches for less than $100.

types of tools can be purchased for a few hundred dollars or less. If you are buying new wrenches, look into the ratchet wrench. When a socket won't fit but you don't want to constantly have to reposition the wrench, the ratchet wrench will cure the problem.

This is not a specific endorsement, but most of my wrenches and sockets are Craftsman. I have used them for years and their lifetime warranty has come in handy more than once. Make sure you have a decent ratchet and socket set. You will definitely need metric sizes if you are building an import tuner, but it is also good to have standard sizes. Typically, I use a ⅜-inch drive and that is sufficient. There are times (the bottom bolts on the rear shocks) I use a ½-inch drive ratchet and sockets and the ¼-inch drive socket. Another nice thing about Craftsman tools is the packages that they offer. For less than $100 you can buy a set that has both metric and standard drive sizes of ¼, ⅜ and ½. That's a pretty good deal if you don't have any tools to begin with. I have acquired lots of tools through the years, usually in assorted brands and sizes. You wouldn't believe how nice it is to have a complete set of sockets and ratchets.

If you use an impact wrench, it is helpful to purchase a set of impact sockets. They are available in shallow or deep design and they withstand the abuse of the impact wrench. I didn't spend a lot of money on these sockets; they were less than $10 a set.

If you are using a compressor and have a few bucks extra, look into buying an air ratchet; it sure makes a quick job of removing bolts and nuts.

It is also worth the money to purchase a set of impact sockets. Impact sockets are usually hardened and withstand the pounding that an impact wrench gives the sockets. I have used regular sockets, but I usually regret it. I have both metric and standard deep and shallow sockets and they take a beating from the impact wrench.

There are a few other helpful tools that are not always included in the prepackaged kits (depending on the kit you buy), but are accessories that you will need, such as 10-inch extensions and a universal or flex joint for the ratchet and sockets.

Other tools are helpful and fun to use, but not necessary. Extendable and flexible magnets and mirrors help find tools and parts that are dropped in hard-to-reach places. It seems that every job has one difficult spot where the nut falls into a location that my fingers can't reach, and often I can't even see it. That's when a mirror and magnet come into play. Sometimes a magnet won't even do the trick and that's when we pull out the flexible fingers. Flexible fingers is a long, flexible shaft that has a small claw-like mechanism that extends from the shaft with the press of a button or trigger. The claw holds nuts and bolts (and almost anything else) that the human arm and fingers just can't reach. You will note in the photos that we used the flexible fingers during the installation of the LSD doors. This was a result of our door kit being packaged with locking nuts instead of rivet nuts.

Remember, always be certain to buy quality tools, and keep them clean and in good condition. Greasy, worn, or

Another luxury tool is a set of combination wrenches that have a ratcheting box end. The ratcheting box end is very useful when you have limited access for the wrench or if you cannot use a socket and ratchet.

dull tools are dangerous. Slippage not only skins the knuckles but it damages the nuts and bolt heads, making future repairs even more difficult.

It is also handy to have a tool bag to carry around tools. If you are working on the car at a friend's or in the driveway and don't want to lug all your tools around, get a small bag or box to carry the stuff you are going to use. I have a Klein Tool bag that I have used for a number of years. It has numerous pockets, handles, and a shoulder strap. It works great when I just want to take enough tools to work on a specific job.

You will also need to own a decent jack, car ramps, and jack stands. Somehow you have to get the car into the air so you can work underneath the vehicle safely. I know a few people who use bottle jacks, but I have always liked a good floor jack. You do not have to buy the top-of-the-line; most hardware stores or auto parts stores have a package that includes a jack and two jack stands for less than $50. Make sure the jack and stands are rated for the weight of your car—usually less than two to three tons is sufficient for most tuner cars. Do not put the car up on a jack without

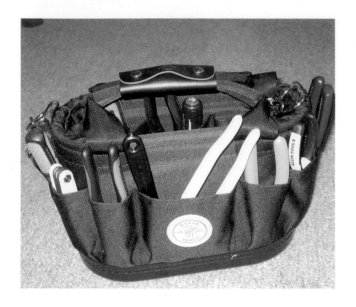

*Left: Klein Tools sells a practical bag to keep your tools handy. I fill this bag with the necessary tools I need for each project. Having a tool bag allows me to do projects in the garage or in the driveway, and not necessarily in my shop. **Right:** A good, quality floor jack and jack stands are necessary to support the car safely. A 2- to 3-ton floor jack can be purchased for less than $40 (and that often includes two jack stands). If you plan to lift both the front and the rear at the same time, you will need to purchase another set of jack stands. You can spend a lot more money on a good floor jack, but it's not necessary when you're working on lightweight tuner cars.*

using jack stands or car ramps. Always block the wheels and use the emergency brake. I used four stands so I could remove the struts and exhaust without having to raise and lower the car.

Jack placement underneath the car is important. Make sure the jack is in a position so it will not tip or roll (like the jack stands), and where you have access to the release and have room to pump the handle. The lifting point needs to be a solid location and big enough that the jack doesn't slip from the location. I keep a couple of scrap pieces of 2x4 around the shop. The wood is used as a spacer on the lift of the jack and sometimes as a cross beam to give the jack a solid lifting position.

It is important to place the jack stands on firm and level ground. Rocks, gravel, dirt or sand allow the jack stands to settle and tip, making the car unsteady and putting you in a very dangerous situation. The same thing can happen with asphalt. If you are working on asphalt, especially on a hot day, the jack stands can sink into the asphalt unevenly. Sometimes it might be necessary to place a square of plywood or even metal or concrete under the jack stands' feet to give them a solid surface. If you jack the front first and place the jack stands under the front of the car, the emergency brake (and blocks behind the rear wheels) will help keep the car from rolling and rocking the jack stands.

After you raise the front, lower the jack slowly and move it to the rear. Slowly jack the rear of the car and always watch the front jack stands to ensure they are not moving

or tipping. Each time I raised the rear, it was always a surprise how much the car would appear to roll. Maybe it was my imagination, but it's important to take all the precautions possible to prevent movement.

SAFETY

It's also important to have someone else help you work on the car anytime you are under the vehicle. Safety is paramount; too many accidents happen when people work alone on their vehicles. Ask a friend to hang out with you while you are working. They don't have to do anything but be there in case you need an extra hand or something happens. If you don't have help, make sure someone knows where you are and checks regularly on you if you are working by yourself.

Sound can be harmful to your ears, whether it is from a vacuum, the engine, or the wind whistling in your ears. Purchase some quality earplugs to protect your hearing. Make sure you get a brand and decibel-reduction rating that is going to work for you.

Always wear eye protection. Power buffers, sanders, and sprayers can throw debris and chemicals back into the operator's eyes. Working under the car creates a situation where dirt and debris can fall into your eyes. Experience and damaged spots on my eyes are proof that eyeglasses or eye protection is valuable.

There are all kinds of mechanics gloves available that will help prevent the scratched knuckles. Some of the gloves

Any time you jack the car, make sure you have jack stands supporting the car. Do not use concrete blocks or blocks of wood; you need to have something that can hold the weight and is a stable support. When working underneath your car, always let someone know where you are, or, better yet, have someone be in the garage with you.

prevent cuts and gouges. Mechanics gloves are good for a lot of jobs, but at times can restrict the ability to pick up washers and small items. Before you buy a pair, try them on and see how flexible they are. Even if you are not using mechanics gloves, it is a good plan to protect your hands from harmful substances. Lightweight rubber gloves can protect your skin when applying chemicals, spraying paint, removing grease, or even cleaning carpets.

Any painting or cleaning can cause fumes that can be hazardous. An appropriate air-filter mask should be worn at all times. Painting and polishing should always be done in a well-ventilated area. Make sure there are no open flames, such as pilot lights and furnaces, in the area where you are painting or when working with the fuel system. Disconnect the battery, and eliminate the risk of fire or explosion. A safety tip: *always* store fuel in approved and appropriately marked containers away from an ignition source. And make sure you have a fire extinguisher handy.

POWER AND POWER TOOLS

You will need a quality indoor-outdoor extension cord—actually, more than one is nice. Make sure the cord and the outlet are both grounded for protection—do not use a cord that has the third grounding plug removed. Keep all cords away from and out of water. If you don't have access to electricity, a few-hundred-watt portable generator will provide most of the power needed for lighting and other electrical tools.

An electric impact wrench is a great tool to help remove tough rusted-on bolts. Depending on the condition of your vehicles, you may need an impact wrench for the exhaust, lug nuts, shocks, and struts or even a fender. If you don't buy or borrow electric impact wrenches, check out an air impact wrench. Air wrenches are often cheaper, but they

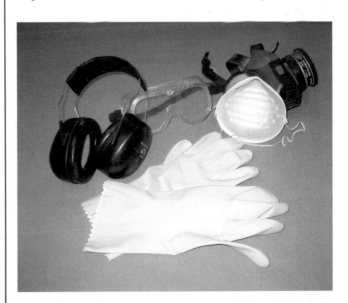

Many people ignore safety when they are working in their own garage. Don't be that person who gets metal fragments in your eyes or ruins your hearing from loud noises. Make sure you wear earplugs or earmuffs, safety glasses or goggles, and gloves when using chemicals.

I have a fairly small compressor—only a couple horsepower with a 15-gallon tank. This size works pretty well for my air ratchet, the limited painting I do, and some minor work with an air chisel. It is not quite big enough to operate an air impact wrench to my satisfaction.

I like cordless tools. The Bosch cordless Tough One is very easy to use because of its smaller size and lighter weight, yet it's powerful enough to do most anything I need, whether I am using it as a drill, grinder, or even a screwdriver.

don't seem to generate the same amount of power as electric models. Of course, that depends a lot on your compressor. Air impacts need a decent flow of air and a large enough tank to keep the pressure on. So be sure to have a quality compressor, and don't forget the impact sockets.

If you do any painting or have an air ratchet or even an air sander, it is necessary to have an air compressor. Compressors cost money, but sometimes using an air tool makes things a whole lot easier. Remember, most air tools have a cousin that's powered by electricity. If you do opt to buy a compressor, you'll probably need to have at least two or three horsepower and a 15- to 20-gallon tank to allow you to do effective touch up painting. In most of my projects, the painting was on small items or small areas and didn't require the complete painting of the car (although I have painted a number of cars with my compressor). Instead of buying a bigger compressor, it might be in your best interest to hire a paint shop if you are to completely paint the car.

CORDLESS TOOLS

As an alternative to corded electric tools, and for matters of convenience, you might consider purchasing a cordless. A good cordless tool kit should include some sort of cordless drill/screwdriver. Bosch Tools makes a very good, compact ⅜-inch, 14.4-volt cordless drill/driver, the Compact Tough.

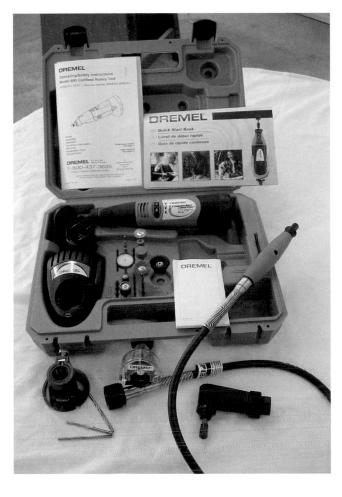

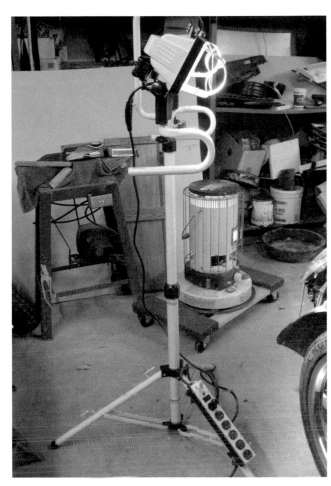

Left: A Dremel cordless tool is another one of my favorite devices. I use it on the car, in my hobbies, and around the house. It has a lot of different attachments, including flexible shafts, cut-out tools, right-hand drives, and more. It can be used to cut out the bumpers on the car for the Razzi kit or grind away at the broken mounts under the hood. Right: Good lighting is very important when working on a project. At today's home-improvement shops, there are a lot of options for halogen lights, especially on stands. This model stands 6-feet tall, has two halogen lights, provides more illumination than you can imagine, and offers a little heat on the cold days.

One big advantage of the Bosch is the smaller size. The 14.4-volt rechargeable battery lasts quite a while, and if you need to charge it, you can connect it to a power converter in your vehicle. Purchase a five-inch hook and loop pad (with the buffing pad and sanding disks) at a hardware store, and you can quickly go from a soft buffing pad to a sanding disk in seconds. You can even buy a cordless impact wrench. I haven't used the cordless impact so I can't give an opinion, but if it works it might make a good alternative.

I also like a small cordless 10.8-volt model Dremel tool that can be used to get into small areas to clean threads, cut off rusted bolts or hoses, or even grind small chips and cracks to prepare them for filling. You can also use a Dremel for cleaning spark plugs, polishing chrome, and cutting holes. Because of the small size of the cordless Dremel, it can be used in a lot of areas that the larger tools can't, and it can even be fitted with additional attachments and used for other jobs for which you would normally need a shop full of tools. The right angle attachment allows you to sand or grind an area that won't allow direct straight-in access of the Dremel. A flex-shaft attachment allows the bit to be maneuvered into hard-to-reach areas. The multipurpose cutting kit turns the Dremel into a rotary saw using a straight bit that allows holes to be made when a circular or jig saw is too big. And Dremel even makes a "mini saw," which has a small saw blade that can be used to cut wood and fiberglass. Rarely have I needed more power than the 10.8-volts the Dremel provides, and I like its simplicity.

LIGHTING

Good lighting is always important to complete a project. Quartz or halogen lights have become very reasonably priced. For less than $40 you can buy two lights mounted on an adjustable stand.

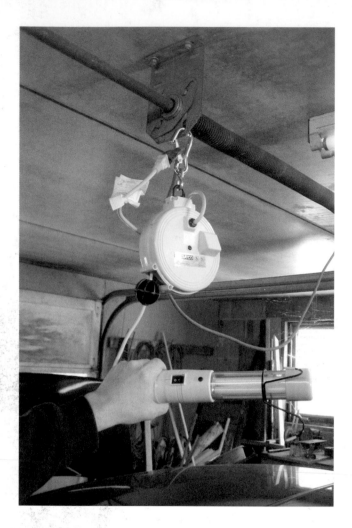

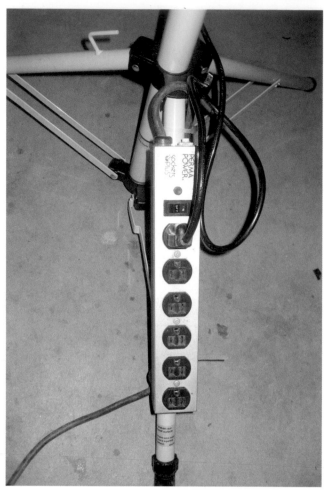

Left: It's important to have a light that you can use in or under the car. I not only have a trouble light on a cord, but I also have a retractable-cord trouble light that is mounted above the car. While the cord is only 20 feet long, it gives me the ability to move around the car and get under the car. When finished with it, all I have to do is pull the cord and it retracts into the case hanging from the ceiling. *Right:* I always seem to have more things to plug in than I have outlets. I mounted a multi-plug to the leg of the light stand using plastic wire ties. I plugged the light into the multi-plug and then I can plug other items into the multi-plug. All I need is one extension cord to the base of the light.

These lights provide a tremendous amount of light and can be adjusted to different heights and angles. In fact, at that price, it is probably worth the money to buy two sets of lights. You can never have too much light. It's also important to have a quality portable trouble light. The florescent tube designs seem to withstand impacts and bumps far better than the old filament light bulb style. It's pretty frustrating to be sliding around under the car and bump or drop the light and you have to stop everything to go get a new bulb. I have also found it handy to add a retractable cord light to the shop. My retractable light has a short 20-foot reach but it is sufficient to stretch around and under the car. I attached a metal snap to the loop on the top of the retractable cords case so that I can connect it above the car on the ceiling of the garage or to a bracket for the garage

door. I have access to the light wherever I am working. Mounting the retractable unit up high helps keep the cord from lying on the ground and getting in the way of the creeper or getting wet from water. If you do hang the light from the ceiling, the cord could drag across the fenders and roof of the car, so be careful where you mount it or it will leave scratches.

EXTRAS

Make sure you have an old soft blanket or a fender protector to put across painted areas that you are leaning over. Be sure that the protector you use does not fall on the floor or get any type of contamination from sand, dirt, or even pilling of the fabric. Any foreign material will leave marks and scratches in the finish of your car. Remove your belt

*Left: If you don't use the multi-plug, you can also buy retractable cords with multiple plugs built-in. This unit cost less than $25. **Right:** While you don't have to have a creeper or a stool, it sure makes it easier on your back if you do. I got this stool on sale at Sears, and even with hydraulic height adjustment, it cost $25.*

and/or your belt buckle. I don't know how many people I know (including myself) who have leaned a little too close to the car and left a scratch from a belt buckle or zipper of a coat. If it is metal and it is unprotected, take it off. Unless you are planning on a repaint, don't take a chance.

Do you have a creeper? It is well worth the money to get a good quality creeper if you are going to be spending much time on your back working on the bottom side of the vehicle. It helps to have an adjustable headrest, but it is not required. I still use the old wooden creeper that's been in my garage for longer than I care to admit. I also have a small mechanics stool available for less than $30 that allows me to get up off my knees and save my back. I might be getting old, but it sure is nice to roll around at comfortable heights and not be in pain.

But I do have to get on the ground, and sometimes the creeper or the mechanics stool just won't work. In those cases I have an old piece of carpet that I lay on the floor. It gives me a little comfort, doesn't roll around and keeps my back from getting cold on the concrete. You can also use floor mats, rubber doormats, or even an old blanket if necessary.

Being well-equipped makes any project go faster and smoother. But remember, you do not have to buy the most elaborate toolbox, biggest compressor or most expensive tools to work on your car. Just make sure they are good quality and you have an assortment. Oh, and it's also helpful to have a number of friends who have more tools than you so you can always borrow as a back-up source.

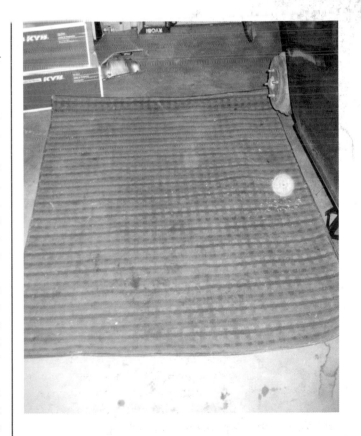

Sometimes even a creeper makes it too hard to get under the car. In that case, use a piece of scrap carpet. The scraps also act as an insulator against often cold-floors. If you don't have a scrap piece of carpet around, you can always buy a remnant from a carpet store.

CHAPTER 2
WHAT IS A TUNER CAR?

When I started this book, I almost forgot to talk about what a "tuner car" was. I grew up in an era when customizing a car entailed chopping, channeling, and installing big block engines. Originally, whenever I thought of building a car, a four-cylinder import engine never crossed my mind. In fact, rarely did a six-cylinder come into view. It was almost always a Chevy, Ford, or Hemi V-8 engine that was the basis for our performance. I always wanted a Barracuda and almost bought a purple 1970 coupe, but didn't think it was a good deal. My older brother owned a 1968 Road Runner, red with a white vinyl top and white leather interior; what a great car. One of my friends from high school still has a 1968 Road Runner, light blue convertible. Growing up, my desire was for Mustangs, Camaros and Chargers. My father's business had a salesman who used to

call on us driving a Plymouth Superbird; you know the one with the long nose and high spoiler/fin on the rear. I never once thought about performance from an import, except for my Volkswagen-powered dune buggy or a Porsche 911. It never dawned on me that I would be using an import engine to develop horsepower as high as a V-8 and that a Honda would be the hot rod of the new generation.

My kids look at Hondas, Mitsubishis, and Toyotas as today's cars. This might have been spurred on by the *Fast and the Furious* movies, but it also appears to be from today's automotive society. Young gear heads are able to buy Hondas and other import cars at reasonable prices, get better economy and longer life than those old-style muscle cars. While the muscle cars may be making a comeback for the baby boomer, they aren't breaking in to the X, Y, or Z

Muscle cars are still among my favorite types of hot rods. Sure, I like Hondas, Toyotas, and Subarus, but I still believe cars like this Camaro will be the true example of a custom car.

Cars like this one, painted with exotic colors and sporting wings and spoilers, are what today's kids see as a sports car. It is their generation's muscle car. The sport compact and tuner car market got a huge boost from the movie the Fast and the Furious.

generations. Who can blame them? When you can build a $5,000 Honda and produce 400 to 600 horsepower, why do you need a Road Runner or Charger?

But what is a tuner? Surprisingly I liked what I found on Wikipedia when I did an Internet search for the definition of a tuner. Wikipedia characterizes the origin of the car as a "sport compact" and then adds the definition of tuner after that. Even if this isn't the best source of definitions, it followed everything I hade ever heard about the tuner car. Following are the two different parts of the definitions. You can make your own choices.

From Wikipedia, the free encyclopedia: *"A sport compact is a high-performance version of a compact car or a subcompact car. [It is] typically front engined, [and examples include] front-wheel-drive coupés, sedans, or hatchbacks driven by a naturally aspirated straight-four gasoline engine. Typical sport compacts include the Acura Integra, Honda Civic, Acura RSX, Toyota Cel-*

ica, Volkswagen GTI, and, more recently, the Dodge Neon SRT-4. The name for any sport compact in a hatchback form is a hot hatch. The design philosophy of a sport compact sharply contrasts with those of 'true' sports cars. Sports cars are designed with a performance-oriented philosophy, often compromising cargo space, seating, gas mileage, (daily) driveability, and reliability. A sport compact is usually designed with a practical design philosophy and profit in mind. This philosophy has led to several compromises when it comes to performance, such as front-wheel-drive, conservative engine design, and platform sharing. Electronic control units are also programmed for optimal gas mileage. Performance-oriented sport compacts focus on improving handling and increasing engine efficiency, rather than increasing engine size or conversion to rear-wheel drive. For example, the Celica GT-S and RSX Type-S are both sport compacts that produce 100 hp/ L of displacement, and have handling superior to their stock trims and other cars in its price range."

Tuners are not always Hondas or Toyotas. In this case, a Mini is an example of a sport compact/tuner. The original Mini Cooper was often customized for performance, looks, and handling.

And a further definition of "tuning" or making a "tuner." "It has become fairly popular to modify or customize a sport compact, commonly referred to as tuning. This has given rise to the term 'tuner' for the owners of modified sport compacts (and other vehicle classes), and by extension, their automobiles. As with trucks and other vehicle categories, there is a large market for performance-enhancing equipment designed to fit small cars. Unfortunately, 'tuning' is a term that is also symbolized by cosmetic and non-performance-related vehicle modifications. It is the subject of some controversy whether to recognize a compact 'tuner' car that has been modified to offer lesser vehicle performance than a 'sport compact'. Restoration of a Japanese import to its JDM specifications (or J-Spec) has become a fairly popular modification for many tuners in North America. It is quite common for Japanese automakers to produce or export less-powerful versions of their models to the North American market. Such modifications usually involve swapping engines and transmissions. Popular examples include the conversion of Nissan 240SX into a Silvia, or a Honda Civic into a Civic Type-R. These modifications can also be cosmetic, such as the replacement of the front fascia or rear spoiler with its JDM counterpart."

Typically a tuner is considered to be an import car that has been modified. There are two versions: those that are modified to look like a fast and sleek car without having anything done to improve the performance, or those that are modified with increased horsepower and improved suspensions and sound systems, but usually without much change in the exterior-looks department. Plain-looking fast cars are "sleepers." Sleepers have been around from the Prohibition days. That's when cars looked slow and old, but had hot rod engines, special springs, and could outrun the lawmen.

For me, the tuner car should have body enhancements, lowering kits and wings, or spoilers. Throw in vertical doors and superchargers and what you have is a modern-day "muscle" car. Just because it doesn't have a big engine, and it doesn't sound like the big block V-8s of the "old" days, they go just as fast.

FINDING THE RIGHT CAR

What's the first thing you do when thinking of building a custom car? Look at what you have to start with. That's exactly what I did. Before I went on the search to buy my next project car, I looked at what was parked in the driveway and whether it would make a good tuner.

In our driveway we had a Ford F250 Super Duty, a 1997 Subaru Outback and a 2003 Mustang convertible. Ford truck as a tuner, I don't think so. The Ford Mustang, maybe . . . but is a Mustang really a tuner? The Mustang is a great car; fun to drive and with rear-wheel drive it would make a great drifter. But I don't think it fits my definition of a tuner car (and it's my wife's).

Remember, when I think of tuners I definitely don't think of V-8 engines. I think of four-cylinder (possibly a six-cylinder) engines hopped up to generate noise and squealing front tires; import cars manufactured by Honda, Toyota, Mitsubishi, and maybe Subaru.

Subaru Outback? Now that was a thought. Our Subaru Outback has performed flawlessly since we bought it. It has

Even though I grew up with a big V-8, and I really like the sound and the power generated, it's amazing how much horsepower can be pulled from a small sport compact engine. Many of the true tuners are generating 600 and 700 horsepower from a small four-or six-cylinder, which is not much different than this big V-8. But the fuel burn on the four- or six-cylinder engine is often lower than the big V-8.

We bought our Subaru Outback in 1997, and it has worked flawlessly. It's all-wheel drive; the horizontally opposed four-cylinder engine generates decent horsepower, high gas mileage and low maintenance. It meets most people's requirements as a tuner, except it is a four-door sport-utility station wagon.

been unstoppable in the winter snow and reliable as kid transportation. It has made a great first car for both of our kids. A Subaru Outback might be an interesting project, sometime, but I was after something with a few more aftermarket performance parts and fewer doors.

So the search was on. The parameters for the project car needed to be established. First, the vehicle has to be plentiful. One advantage to a car that has market numbers is that you usually have lots of aftermarket parts available. It seems to be a numbers game in almost everything we do. The more popular a car and the more of a certain model sold, the more aftermarket parts and modifications are available for that model. The more extras that are available for that particular model of car, the more reasonable the prices seem to be (not only the cars, but also the aftermarket parts).

This sport compact is just one example of what's possible. But with its vertical doors, plastic seats, and exotic sound system, it is more expensive than what our budget tuner will ever be.

There is always one last big requirement for anything I own. Whatever the vehicle choice, it also has to look good and be fun to drive. Not surprisingly, for many people, that might be a bigger factor than any of the other items. Many cars look good but don't really perform or operate as well as they could (or should). And lastly, it has to meet the approval of my teenage daughter who wants to be able to drive the car before, during, and after the modifications.

After I find a car that meets those basic guidelines, what do I want to achieve with a cheap tuner? It could be the speed, the power, or the noise from the bass-thumping speakers in the trunk that I was looking for. Maybe it would be acknowledgment and admiration from pedestrians and other drivers who see the car. There are so many options for a car nut to consider.

In reality, the audio was the least of my worries and last on my list for completion, if I attacked that at all. I would

have to say increasing horsepower and handling would be the starting point. I wanted something that was bolt-on horsepower and handling. Simple improvements at a cheap cost are the whole premise of the book. And don't forget, even though I want horsepower and handling changes, it has to be teenager manageable. That also means I want something that provides reliable horsepower. I don't need high-performance internal parts unless they will provide manageable and reliable in-town performance. Besides, this is a "tuner on a budget," which also means the less teardown I have to do and the less time I spend working on the car, the better the value for the mile I get.

Originally I was thinking about the Dodge Neon. I noticed many of the older models had peeling paint and a few other minor problems. These minor discrepancies also made the Neon plentiful. Plus there were two and four doors, sport- and plain-trim models, automatic, stick shift,

If you have an opportunity to buy a Honda SI, you will get a double overhead cam VTEC engine, which is even better to start with than a standard VTEC single overhead cam engine. You also get the SI extras that make the modification process go faster.

sunroofs, and still, most of the used Neons were reasonably priced. I even spent a cold morning at a local car dealer holding my hand on the hood of a used Neon. This was one of those dealer sales shenanigans. Hold your hand on the car, the sales manager writes the ridiculously low price on the windshield and you get to buy the car for that amount. In my case, the price wasn't ridiculous enough for a project car, so I kept on looking. After all of this, a decision was made that the Neon just didn't seem to have the look desired for the book. Sure it was a basic, cheap car, but it lacked the pizzazz I was hoping for.

The search continued. Mitsubishi makes a number of cars that meet my needs; one in particular that my daughter liked was the Eclipse. The Eclipse has actually become quite popular in the tuner circuit. This is also why the prices were higher than I wanted to spend. I also looked at the Nissan's 240 with rear-wheel drive. The 240 would make a

great drifter car. But, we aren't building a car just for me to drive, so drifting isn't on my list as a "must have" performance capability.

Mazda has a few options, one of which is the RX7. It's not always considered a tuner but it's fun to drive with lots of potential. Jeanne and I have owned five RX7s and never had a bad experience or a bad drive! I did own a Miata for awhile and gave a quick thought to searching for one, but that didn't take either. My idea of a Miata project is to put a five-liter small block V-8 in for the performance improvement. Remember the Monster Miata?

Volkswagen, Subaru, and even Pontiac models came up as potential. Cars such as the Jetta, Golf, and Vibe have a niche but they were pretty expensive to start with.

Conversations with friends, tuner car owners, and the editor revealed what we all probably knew from the beginning: start with a Honda. Honda will probably always be

If you're lucky enough to find a car like this, you'll be half way to the tuner finish line. This Civic has the Razzi ground effects kit and larger wheels and tires. Photo courtesy of Razzi

considered the first of the tuner category. The Civic, Accord, and Prelude all make great starter cars. They are economical to buy, cheap to operate, and have lots of aftermarket parts available.

Civic is one of the most plentiful on the market. The Civic can be found in hatchback, coupe, and four-door configurations. I started looking for a two-door coupe with the V-tech engine and the SI package—which wasn't as easy as I hoped. Oh, they were available for sale. There were SI cars from the late 1990s that had a few mods done already. Most of the older SIs averaged around 100,000 miles and were priced at about $1,000 or more above the EX models. For example, I found a 2000 Civic SI, well equipped and in good condition for $7,500. But in comparison, I also found a 2002 Civic EX for less than $5,000. Both were fully equipped five speeds and had similar mileage. Sure I lost the SI extras, but the money I would save on the purchase allowed the addition of a few more extras to the car. So, I bought the EX.

Originally the actual year didn't matter to me. Many of the early 1990s cars were cheaper and partially modified and I thought I might buy one of those. But once I started shopping I narrowed my search down to a 1997 up to maybe a 2003 vehicle. The later models were picked mostly because I wanted additional safety equipment that was offered in the later years. I also did a number of web searches to see changes in the Civics lineage. Good sites for that were www.edmunds.com and the Honda website.

I also looked up websites that gave advice about the car I chose, and even the modifications that I planned on installing. Owners' groups are a great source of information. You can get tips and tricks that have worked for people just like you, on cars just like yours—a great thing to have available. No more waiting for the next issue of the newsletter or looking for a book at a swap meet. The Internet has made joining these groups and keeping up on model specific information as easy as clicking a mouse. All it takes is a little time and an Internet connection and you can gain access to a number of forums and websites with all kinds of tips and advice.

In my search of the Worldwide Web, I learned that the 1998- to 2002-model Honda Civics included a 1.6-liter, 106-horsepower engine in the CX, DX, and LX, and a slightly more powerful 1.7 liter, 127-horsepower VTEC-assisted version in the EX models. Well, of course, we wanted as much horsepower as possible to start with so the EX was the choice. Plus, if you add in Hondas basic summary of the seventh-generation (2000) Civic, you'll find more room, better safety, and smoother rides. I felt that of all the different years available, the late 1990s to early 2000 vehicles had a lot to offer. Besides, my teenage daughter didn't like the looks of the hatchback or the older-model Civics. Her opinion, although not the only one, was used to help make the model decision.

Where can you find the perfect budget tuner car? In a word: anywhere. That's right, if you are looking for a good buy, don't be afraid to shop all over the country. Use the Internet if you have it. Before the Internet I would go to the local library and look at the local newspaper and the newspapers from major metropolitan areas (such as the Los Angeles Times) around the country. These days, most community libraries have computer and Internet access. You will be surprised at the number of cars for sale. It's the law of numbers. More people, more cars.

I started my Honda Civic search with the classified section in the local paper and online. Many of today's newspapers have an online section or they are connected to an Internet classified service such as Cars.com. Locally, I was able to find a couple of cars that initially looked like they met my needs. After a little more research and asking my questions, I narrowed that down to one car to look at locally.

Let me make a side note here. What I hate the most about searching for cars is leaving messages and not getting answers. I guess it's a pet peeve of mine. If you have an ad in the paper (or anywhere for that matter) and you put a phone number in the ad, answer the phone or return the calls. If you already have sold the car, cancel the ad or call back the interested parties and tell them the car is sold. I do not know how many ads I called in which I was unable to get an answer or I left a message and didn't get a call back.

Back to the search. As I was working the local area, I logged on to a couple of Honda websites and started to

LONG DISTANCE BUYING

I've bought from local, private sellers and in neighboring states where I have driven to pick up the vehicles. I have also found cars where I needed to fly to a location. Long-distance buying can be fun, but expensive. I still remember buying a Jaguar XJS in Texas and driving it back to Iowa. The car worked great for the first hour. After that, the trip was an experience in British electronics and ignition systems. Even though I knew the reputation of Jaguar electrics and was—I thought—prepared for any problems, I never expected the extra five-plus hours it took for the trip. What started out as a great deal ended up being my first Jaguar V-8 conversion. Ultimately, I still had a great looking, fun-to-drive car.

If you plan on buying out of state, make sure that you figure in the travel expenses and the risks. Whether you fly or drive, it costs money to go pick up a car. I typically add about $1,000 to a purchase if I have to go very far out of town. Typically I buy a round-trip airline ticket (just in case I don't like what I see) and plan on fuel and expenses on the return trip. A number of years back, a friend and I flew to Los Angeles to buy a drivable but damaged car. We left there late in the day and wanted to get out of town quickly. We drove straight through from L.A. back to Iowa in about 24 hours. That was years ago when I could stay up past 10 at night and not worry about speeding tickets. With the two of us we were able to fly out, drive back, and eat fast food for less than $1,000, and that included a speeding ticket on the east edge of California (who would have thought a little old Mustang CHIPs car would catch us in a Porsche Turbo 924?).

One thing I don't like is taking the bus. Sure the bus can be cheaper and easier on the driver, but it can also be miserable. My wife, Jeanne, and I once made a trip between Kansas City and our home to deliver a car. This was a trip that would usually take between three and four hours, one way. But on the bus it took us eight hours! We stopped at every small town and even had a stop for lunch and fuel.

I still travel around the country on a regular basis. I am usually on the East and West Coasts a couple of times a year and assorted stops throughout the rest of the nation. At this stage in my life if I can't fly, I drive. Some people think it's crazy, but I like to drive. Plus, I like to shop for cars, bikes, planes, boats, and ukuleles while I am traveling. Bus drivers and airlines don't make very many sudden stops to check out that old car in a hay field, but I do.

There are advantages of looking for a car on the Internet, among them the access to color pictures and e-mail to communicate with the seller.

track the "for sale" ads. By watching ads from around the country I was able to start building my price guidelines. I did that by comparing condition, mileage, and prices. I wanted to establish what I felt were my base numbers for a Honda Civic EX. By calling and e-mailing a few of the ads, I was able to get a feel for the condition of the vehicles. I ended up calculating that I needed to buy a 1997 or later vehicle and I wanted to spend $2,500 to $7,000. That price range should get me a very nice vehicle.

The advantage of an Internet search is pictures. If pictures were not available and/or the owner didn't want to send pictures, I wasn't interested in the car (especially if it was a long-distance purchase). Digital pictures and the Internet have been lifesavers in searching for cars across the country.

Building on a budget puts a new perspective on buying a car. It changes "what you want" into "what you can afford." There is more to building a tuner than just buying the car. The parts are what start to add up; the budget tuner has to be based on the total package. In some cases there are cars that already include a few items, such as custom wheels or exhaust. Others already have ground effect packages installed. One way to keep the cost down is to buy a car that someone has already started but didn't have time or money to finish. If the modifications follow your plans, go for it.

As you start looking for cars, be sure to document the process. Begin with the search, outlining price parameters, questions to ask when talking to sellers, etc. In fact, practice calling a few ads to see what kind of answers you get. If you can develop a series of basic questions, you can eliminate a number of the ads very quickly. This helps narrow

down the search to the best prospects. Then, when you actually start looking at the viable candidates in person, the vehicle will be "pre-approved," in a sense. Watch out for the "pre-purchase pitfalls" especially if buying online. One way to do that is to ask lots of questions.

What kinds of questions should you ask? Well, it depends. Usually, the ad will give the basics, prompting a phone call. Many sellers list the model, extras, and maybe even mileage. But after that I want to know how long the seller has owned the car. I figure if the seller hasn't owned the car very long he or she doesn't know as much of the history. The next topic I discuss is damage history. Damage history—minor or major, it doesn't matter, I just want to know. Remember, most states still do not require reporting of any damage unless it's over a certain dollar amount. Personally, I'll take major damage history if it's been repaired and recorded accurately, and, almost as important, if it is priced accordingly.

Have you ever used CARFAX? If not, you should. By using the vehicle's unique vehicle identification number (VIN), CARFAX records a history on cars and trucks. According to the CARFAX website:

"CARFAX Vehicle History Reports provide information that can impact a consumer's decision about a used car or truck. A CARFAX Report may include:

Title information, including salvaged or junked titles
Flood damage history
Total loss accident history
Odometer readings
Lemon history
State emissions inspection results
Number of owners
Service records
Lien activity, and/or
Vehicle use (taxi, rental, lease, etc.)"

That's a lot of nice information and great to have before you spend the money and buy the car. While this is not a perfect system to track the car's history, it sure helps. If the owner has had the car for a long time you can probably glean the information from him or her if you can talk long enough. If it's a dealer, CARFAX might be your best hope (besides a good inspection by a mechanic). But if the car is rough and cheap, you probably can expect damage history and minor problems. After you get done doing the modifications it will be worth more money anyway!

Opposite: If you've never used CARFAX, it's well worth it. Even though I knew this vehicle was a rebuilt salvage, I was able to confirm where it was from and when it was wrecked. I also used CARFAX to check on a couple of other cars I was shopping for. I signed up for the service over a period of time and CARFAX allowed me to make as many VIN checks as I needed during that time period.

ORDER REPORTS | FIND A CAR | REGISTER GUARANTEE | ABOUT US | HELP | LOGIN | HOME

No Risk - 100% Guaranteed

Start My Order Now

You can always cancel later

CARFAX® Vehicle History Report™

carfax.com

An independent company established in 1986

2003 HONDA ACCORD EX

1HGCM82633A004352
COUPE
3.0L V6 SFI SOHC 24V / FRONT WHEEL DRIVE
Standard Equipment | Safety Options
CARFAX Safety & Reliability Report
Honda Certified Used Car - 01/03/2007

Hi-I'm the CARFAX Xpert™. I'm here to help you better understand the data in this CARFAX Report. Did you know...

- We checked over 4 billion records from thousands of public and private sources for this vehicle
- This vehicle qualifies for the CARFAX Buyback Guarantee
- The last reported odometer reading was 46,740

SUMMARY

A CARFAX Vehicle History Report is based only on information supplied to CARFAX. Other information about this vehicle, including problems, may not have been reported to CARFAX. Use this report as one important tool, along with a vehicle inspection and test drive, to make a better decision about your next used car.

OWNERSHIP HISTORY
The number of owners is estimated by CARFAX

	OWNER 1
Year purchased	2002
Type of owner	Personal
Estimated length of ownership	4 yrs. 1 mo.
Owned in the following states/provinces	Pennsylvania
Estimated miles driven per year	11,315/yr
Last reported odometer reading	46,740

CARFAX 1 OWNER

TITLE PROBLEMS
CARFAX guarantees the information in this section

	OWNER 1
Salvage	Junk	Rebuilt	Guaranteed No Problem
Fire/Flood	Hail Damage	Buyback/Lemon	Guaranteed No Problem
Not Actual Mileage	Exceeds Mechanical Limits	Guaranteed No Problem

GUARANTEED - None of these major title problems were reported by a state Department of Motor Vehicles (DMV). If you find that any of these title problems were reported by a DMV and not included in this report, CARFAX will buy this vehicle back.

Register | View Terms

OTHER INFORMATION
Not all accidents or other issues are reported to CARFAX

	OWNER 1
Total Loss Check No total loss reported to CARFAX.	✓ No Issues Reported
Frame Damage Check No frame damage reported to CARFAX.	✓ No Issues Reported
Airbag Deployment Check No airbag deployment reported to CARFAX.	✓ No Issues Reported
Odometer Rollback Check No indication of an odometer rollback.	✓ No Issues Indicated
Accident Check No accidents reported to CARFAX.	✓ No Issues Reported
Manufacturer Recall Check Check with an authorized Honda dealer for any open recalls.	✓ No Recalls Reported
Basic Warranty Check Original warranty estimated to have expired. View Info	**Warranty Expired**

Tell us what you know about this vehicle

CARFAX Hot Listings®

Looking for other 2003 HONDA ACCORD vehicles like this one in your area?
Search CARFAX Hot Listings for an up-to-date list of vehicles in your area, all with the CARFAX Buyback Guarantee!

My daughter really wanted a car that included pink. But this paint job was just too ugly for me. I understand somebody had to like this car, but it wasn't a paint scheme that I could get accustomed to.

I am also concerned with the mileage. The type of miles is a factor. Typically, the feeling has always been that highway miles are less strenuous than around-town miles. But in-town miles also depend on what "in-town" means. Stop-and-go commuter freeway miles in a major metropolitan area aren't any better than stop-and-go around a small town, and maybe worse. Why are we worried about mileage if the car is well-maintained? If I want to pump more horsepower out of a stock engine with bolt-on parts, I want to start with an engine that is in good shape, and I want to plan accordingly depending on the history.

Other items to ask about include whether it is an original engine and drive train, what modifications have been completed so far, has the car been smoked in, and even have the carpets and seats been changed?

One item that I always ask at the very start is what color the car is. I, personally, am kind of particular in that area. I don't like green cars and I don't like to keep black cars clean (although I like black cars). I also like primary colors like blue, yellow and red. Red is an aggressive color and has typically maintained a good resale value. Although I hope for red, I will take almost any color . . . except green. (And that's a long story having to do with green motorcycles, green cars, and a couple of unfortunate accidents.)

After all your questions have been answered to your satisfaction, make arrangements to look at the car. If you want to be consistent, create a list of your questions and make copies of it, and give yourself a place to check off the questions and write notes. If you do all of this right, you should be able to eliminate the majority of the ads and cut down on the expenses of shopping for a car.

Too much work? Some people might think that using a checklist and going through all these "hoops" is just a big waste of time. How many people have ever bought a car with a checklist? What about the savings a buyer can get by not spending good money on a bad car? The idea is to get the best possible car for the least amount of money and that means having a plan, using a checklist, and being consistent in the search. Planning and checklists make the process constant and keep the buyer from getting caught up in the emotions of building a dream car.

In all your research you have to reject a few cars to feel good about the one you finally buy. Why reject certain cars and accept others? A lot of the reasoning is personal pref-

erence and gut feelings. If I look at a car and I do not like the looks or the person selling the car, I might be turned off by it. I looked at a 1999 EX, two-door, five-speed, with 145,000 miles. This car was priced at $4,900 in the paper and it was just across town. Not bad for my first inspection. The seller was personable and the car sounded just about like what I wanted. But when I finally looked at the car, it was a little worse than represented, in my opinion. It had a lot of things I didn't like. It had a door that wouldn't open from the inside, a decent-sized dent in a quarter panel, carpet that was greasy, and recently had the radio stolen from the dash (which damaged the dash). (Besides it was a variation of green, which I suppose I could have tolerated if that was all that was wrong.)

None of these items would have been a deal killer by themselves. I had plans to change most of the things anyway, except the door handle problem, but it was the combination of all of them and the price that stopped me from

Even after you ask all the questions, the car might not be what you think. In this case the owner neglected to tell us the stereo had been stolen and the dash damaged. This car also had a wrinkle in the fender, a filthy interior, and a driver's door that would not open from the outside. Yet the owner still wanted a retail price for the car.

buying the car. My target price for that car, sight unseen, was about $4,500. Again, asking price was $4,900 and I was prepared to pay cash. I was also willing to pay more for a car that was local. But after viewing the car, I figured the car was worth about $3,900. Seems low but when you go online and run the numbers in Kelley Blue Book or NADA, $3,900 was a fair price. But not fair enough for the seller. I never even made him an offer

If you don't have a good feeling about the car, and the seller says there are others who are willing to pay them the price they are advertising, then let others make their mistakes.

What is it about car sales? Used, new, dealers, individuals, there is some sort of unwritten law that says we have to price-haggle before we buy the vehicle. True, it is fun to negotiate, in a masochistic sort of way. And I like a bargain, but I also get tired of bargaining.

My method is to figure out what I think the vehicle is worth and how much I am going to offer the buyer. I believe that if I am comfortable with the price I want to pay and I buy the car for the price I agree on, then it's a good deal. Is that more than you would pay? Less than the dealer would pay? Could you buy it for less somewhere else? I am known for having buyer remorse the minute I close a deal. But, by then it's too late. If you make an offer and the offer is accepted, you should be satisfied with the offer. Be happy. Stop worrying about the price and accept the deal.

That's different than buying the vehicle and finding that the seller provided inaccurate information or that the car was misrepresented. Being misled and "cheated" is not a good deal. But that is why it is important to use CARFAX, do your research, and even hire a mechanic if necessary to inspect the vehicle before you buy it.

That is unless the deal is so good, even if it's not quite what you thought, it is still a good deal. Like finding a 2000 Honda Civic SI, 20,000 miles, only driven on Sundays, stored in a heated garage, and the seller only wants $100. We've probably all heard those stories, but most are nothing more than an automotive myth. All I can say is good luck on finding a car like that. If those deals do really exist, it is only once and a while, and it won't last long.

The car I ended up with was simple to acquire. It was advertised in the local Sunday newspaper. I called the seller, made arrangements to look at the car, and drove two hours to view it. While I was asking all my questions, the seller informed me that the car had a salvage title, needed minor repairs, and was being priced accordingly. And surprisingly, it was just like he said.

The car was clean overall. It had some dirt in the carpets, a chip in the windshield and needed some minor work on a bumper. The asking price was half of "book" retail,

which I thought we could make up by adding the extra parts to it to when we make it a tuner car. Before I looked at this car I ordered a CARFAX report to confirm the salvage title, and also find a history of where the car might have been. I discovered it was a Midwest car, which I thought was a good deal. While it wasn't perfect, it was a great car to start with. I did try offering less money. The seller was asking $5,000, and we ended up at $4,800. Yes, there were other cars cheaper than this with more equipment and more miles, and still other cars that were higher priced than this car with lower miles. But this was close, available, and within my budget.

If at all possible, I try to use cash in my hand to negotiate the price. Many times the seller will give me a little better deal if I bring a stack of $100 bills. (Though that's not always the case and I am definitely not recommending that you travel around the country with wads of bills in your pockets.) It has worked for me on a number of cases. I bring bills, I ask for a better price and the seller looks at the stack of money and he/she lowers the price a little. This works best if the car doesn't have a lien that needs to be paid off.

Another little trick that has worked is taking a cashier's check and cash. For example: Say I am looking at a car that has an asking price of $5,000 but I figure it is worth about $4,200. If the seller is accepting a cashier's check, I'll take the check written out for $4,000 and cash to make up the difference. This gives me $1,000 dollars (cash) to negotiate with. Plus, if I am traveling, I am not carrying a huge amount of cash around in my pocket.

In the case of a lien, I like to see if I can pay the payoff price. Sometimes if the loan payoff is close to my price, I offer the payoff amount. In those cases I'll also offer to go to the bank and pay off the vehicle with the seller. The key is being in control of the situation.

Most of us shop for our cars on the weekends. The problem is, unless you are working with a dealer or a company that offers financing, you can't always access the banks on the weekends. Even though it is a little harder to schedule, if you can make the deal happen on a weekday during business hours, you can always access a bank or credit union, and even a mechanic. It is not a requirement, but it helps.

One year I took a late evening flight from Iowa to Burbank, California, to buy a Porsche that had been vandalized. It was simple damage (someone had spent time jumping on the hood). I met the seller at the airport and we negotiated the car deal right there. By the time I had inspected the car, paid the seller, collected all the paperwork (title and a bill of sale), and started my trip back home it was after midnight. There were not many (read that as any!) banks open that late at night.

THE CASE OF THE MISSING TITLE

I thought I found a 2000 Civic SI. The car had 110,000 miles and all the options, plus it was the SI and it was a light blue. It had everything going for it, except that it was overpriced and missing a title. I didn't know the title was missing until it came time to front the money and pay for the vehicle. The seller was unable to provide a title because the title was at a bank in a different state. The seller stated he was selling the car for a relative and as soon as I sent him the money he would be able to pay the bank off and get a title. I was suspicious. I didn't want to give up the money without getting the title at the same time I picked up the car. I had all these thoughts going through my head—like stolen or damaged. When I went to pick up "my" car, would it be anything like the pictures? How did I know he didn't send me pictures of a friend's car and is selling me a pile of parts in the back yard? That's a risk I was really uncomfortable with.

I really wanted this Civic SI. This car met all my requirements as a tuner, except a clear title—it had a lien on it. This SI was a nice SI Blue color and a no-damage history-vehicle. It was priced higher than I wanted to spend, but because it was an SI, I was willing to spend the money.

In this instance the seller would not agree to anything but me sending the money directly to the bank and then I could pick up the car—a five-hour drive. I finally got the seller to give me the bank phone number and I called the bank directly to see if I could pay off the loan. They wouldn't talk too much about the loan and payoff since I wasn't the person on the account. But they would confirm that I could pay off the loan directly if I wanted to, but, they would send the title to the owner who is not the guy I was buying the car from. The seller said it was his nephew who owned the car and he would get the title for me before I showed up for the car. But how did I know it was a good car? How would I know I didn't send my money to the bank and not get anything in return? The problem was whether I would actually get the car I saw in the pictures. Instead of taking a chance, I agreed to pay the asking price if he would get a clear title prior to me looking at the car. He wouldn't. I didn't. So that deal ended and the search continued.

The Datsun 240Z, 260Z, or 280Z would make great drifter cars since they are rear-wheel drive—that is, if you can find a good one. The two-plus-two models are a little long, so stick to the standard model. The hardest part is finding one that's not rusted out.

This Porsche purchase is a great example of doing all my homework early. I had worked with the seller and was guaranteed clear title, arranged the acceptable payment, and carried cash to negotiate with after I arrived. I had numerous pictures of the car from different angles, a picture of the VIN number, a faxed copy of the title, and few other details that made this an almost effortless purchase. My expenses including the round-trip ticket and the drive home were very reasonable—that is except for the speeding ticket heading out of California. When I got home with the Porsche I put a new hood on the car and drove it for a couple months. I was able to sell the car and make about $2,000 . . . even after the ticket.

Not all deals make money, and not all cars have been the right choice. But, if you do the research and don't get impatient, you can win more times than you lose. I believe that buying at a fair and reasonable price and getting a good solid vehicle is what it is really all about.

A quick 10-step summary of the purchase process:

1. Use a checklist to ask the seller a series of questions.
2. Start calling about locally advertised cars and expand the calling radius.
3. If possible, get digital pictures to save you time and travel costs.
4. Order a CARFAX report to research the history.
5. Establish the price you will pay using automotive price guides, Internet ads, and newspaper ads.
6. Inspect and drive the car. (Take to a mechanic if you are uncomfortable inspecting the car yourself).
7. Negotiate the final price.
8. Make arrangements to pay for the car (bank loan, cashier's check, cash, etc.).
9. Pay for the vehicle and get a bill of sale.
10. Drive your new car home!

CHAPTER 3
INSPECTING THE CAR

If at all possible, inspect the car before you buy it. Sometimes that might mean hiring a mechanic and sometimes it might be just looking over the car yourself. If the price is right, I might not always worry about a detailed inspection. In this case, the car had a salvage title and the price was right, so even if it had a few problems, I wasn't too worried. But I was interested in how well it had been repaired.

I started with an external inspection of the body panel and door gaps. Hopefully the shop that rebuilt the car had aligned most of the components accurately.

Our car had a few minor issues. The steering wheel was not straight while the car was driving straight. Not a big issue, but it would require an adjustment. The hood was lower than one fender and a bumper skin would not stay attached to the bumper clip. These are all indications that the front end, even though repaired on a frame machine, was not quite right. It could have been the bending and repair of the frame that was not perfect, or it could be the brackets under the parts. There is no real way to find out

until some of the parts are removed. Looking at the car with a flashlight indicated that the brackets were not bad, so the car was just not put back together exactly right. For me, this wasn't a problem; I figured I could make enough adjustments to the vehicle parts during the reassembly.

During the inspection I also noticed a few other items such as broken brackets and holes in the resonator box. I was planning on to replace the intake anyway, so I didn't worry about the parts, but I was concerned about the level of repairs I was running into. I also noticed a few joints with a lot of sealer covering them. Gaps that weren't quite right and a few wrinkles in the sheet metal also were present.

Okay, so it wasn't a perfect car, but after looking under the car and at the way the doors fit and the way the car drove, I decided to go for it. Not everyone would agree. I have rebuilt a number of wrecked cars and felt comfortable with what I saw. If you are not familiar with salvage cars or "rebuilders," it would be in your best interest to take the car to a shop and have someone else inspect it.

Start your inspection with a quick walk around the car. Check the front for nicks, chips, and any other visible damage.

31

As you look at the rear of the car, check for gaps between the trunk lid and the fenders and the bumpers. Look for signs of oil, soot, or moisture around the tailpipe. You might also look under the car for any signs of damage, rust, or corrosion.

The grille on this car was not fit correctly and did not stay in place. When I test-drove the car the grille flipped up on the hood.

Notice the hood and fender joint. The adjustment on the hood was too low to line up with the fender. This was something minor that could be corrected after installing the LSD doors and reattaching the fenders.

Here's another example of how the car was not fitted correctly. The bumper skin doesn't clip to the fender tightly and stay in place.

The windshield has what appears to be a chip, which has expanded into a crack. We would have to change the windshield after we got the door and the rest of the car finished.

33

The seats and interior were in really good condition except for a few minor stains and dirt.

Left: Good thing we're putting on new tires and wheels, these tires are almost worn out!
Right: The carpets in the car were in need of stain removal and cleaning. I planned to install diamond plate aluminum floor mats from Performance Import Trends, so I wasn't too worried about it. **Lower right:** It's nice to see door panels that are not damaged, cracked, or faded. Both doors fit very well and closed without any problems. The power windows and power locks worked on both doors.

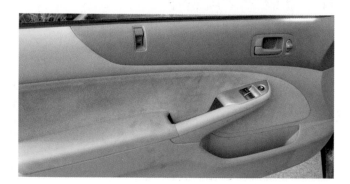

Above: During inspection I used my floor jack to raise the car to look underneath. I was looking for signs of damage that might not have been repaired or signaled how well it was repaired. *Left:* The loose grille was attached with two small sheet metal screws at the top. The bottom of the grille had small tabs that fit into tabs on the bumper. The grille was not attached at the bottom and flexed while driving, and actually bent back up over the hood.

Right: Under the hood, I was looking for signs of damage, leakage, or missing parts. With the way the rest of the car looked, I expected a few problems that might have been left unrepaired after the rebuild.

Below left: Notice the front tower bolts and how rusty they are. This was an indication to me that the car had been exposed to the elements for a while. It also meant we may have had a little difficulty removing some of these bolts and nuts. This is a good time to start a shopping list of what you might need and make sure it includes a rust-penetrating spray, such as Liquid Wrench.

Below right: If you look close, you can see where this portion of the frame was straightened and not replaced. There is a wrinkle visible from the inside of the hood. It will be interesting to see how wrinkled the area is from the outside after removing the fender.

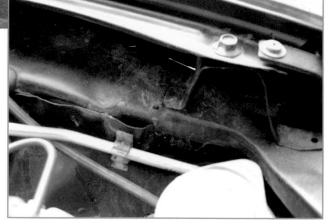

Left: Since this car has damaged in the front, it would be a good idea to look at all the linkage and any components that might have been damaged. The linkage was in good condition, except for a little rust. The front end did have new parts (such as the axles) installed during the rebuild. Housings, hoses, and cables looked to be original.

Below left: There was one spot on the engine that looked like it had been welded. There were no signs of leakage, and the weld appeared to be doing its job. I would have liked it to be a new part, but welding goes along with the rest of the repairs that were made.

Below right: Again, damage signs that the car was left alone. This electrical box has most of its brackets damaged or broken..

Left: The battery was held in place with a piece of wire. This will definitely need to be replaced with the correct brackets. *Right:* More concerns were with any of the accessories that looked original but could have been damaged. The air conditioner compressor looked to be in good condition with only a few scratches in the finish.

I decided to remove the air cleaner cover and inspect the intake and back side of the engine compartment. With the car's history of front-end damage, it could have possibly pushed the engine back into the firewall, and I wanted to inspect that area. The firewall was difficult to see without removing the air cleaner and the air intake resonator box.

The cover of the air cleaner is removed with six screws that are hex (and Phillips) head. I removed the screws and the air cleaner cover before I could remove the air cleaner and the air cleaner housing.

Above: After removing the cover and the air cleaner, you can remove the housing. Note the sensor unit on the driver side of the housing and the breather tube at the front. Once the housing and resonator are removed there is quite a bit of room to look at the firewall and the back side of the engine.

Below left: More signs of unrepaired damage. This could be part of the reason that the fender, bumper, and hood alignment is off.

Below right: More unrepaired damage on the front of the passenger side. This definitely could be why the fenders were not aligning correctly. Since the car was put on a frame machine and aligned during the rebuild, I do not plan on changing the damaged parts. But it may necessitate adding shims under the fenders and hoods to get the gaps and edges to align.

 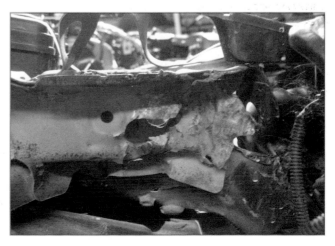

CHAPTER 4
BOUGHT THE CAR, WHAT NOW?

Before you decide on the parts to buy and install, figure out what you are capable of and where you are going to do the work. If you live in the northern states, it might not be practical to start the modifications in the late summer or fall unless you have a garage space to work in. The idea behind this book was to be able to build a car without a lot of special tools or a fancy workshop. Having a car to drive while you work on the tuner makes it easier to start the more difficult modifications. While none of the mods in this book are really difficult, they could keep the car down for a couple of days if you need more parts, break a piece, or if you don't have time to finish the project. Being able to leave the car on jack stands and torn apart makes a big difference in how much you get done each time you work on the car.

Originally I was offered a spot in a custom shop to do the work. The only problem was that I would be required to push the car out if they needed the space for a customer car—a possibility each night. The manager of the shop liked to make sure his customers cars were in overnight, which I certainly agreed with. But that meant my car had to be on wheels and rollable, not something I wanted to worry about each time I worked on the car.

Another friend offered his warehouse. He put in new lights and made it available whenever I was ready. I opted out of that partly because I would be in the middle of his company's normal operating hours. Late night would require him providing an extra key or leaving me to lock up the place. I wasn't sure I really wanted that responsibility. Plus, his warehouse is not easily accessible if I needed to run out quickly and buy a few additional parts. And lastly, he had a couple of gear heads working in the warehouse who would probably be sidetracked by me working on the car. The upside is they were willing to help me if I needed the extra hands.

I finally decided to clean my own shop and use it. I have a double-garage workshop that has room for toolboxes, a work bench, and the car. It is also filled with everything I never wanted to throw away. My wife calls me a "pack rat." I like to keep lots of items just in case I might ever need them again.

I actually had to build a storage building to house the lawn mowers, assorted tools, and equipment that I owned if I wanted to work on a car. I just didn't have enough room to get the car in if I continued to use the space as a storage facility. But now that it was cleaned out, I started thinking that after the tuner car there might be a custom bike in the works. You know once you have the room, it is hard not to imagine all the other things you can build.

Even with the few items that appeared to be unrepaired, I still thought the car was a good deal. Now I am the proud owner of a 2002 Honda Civic EX. Sure it has a few problems, but by the time I am done adding my parts and the extras it will look like a different car.

I don't have a huge shop, but it is big enough to do most projects that I tackle. My shop is a double-car garage space that has a one-car garage door. The one problem I will have is lifting the vertical doors to a full and upright position with the car on the jack stands—my ceiling is just too low, which is one reason I don't have a car lift. But the doors will open completely when the car is on the ground, on its own wheels.

While my shop is not a huge, elaborately equipped shop, it does have a few things going for it. It has a 220 panel installed, a small compressor, and a 110-volt stick welder. I have a small table-top metal bender, spot welder, bench vice, overhead fluorescent lights, and a halogen light stand. I also have a 2½-ton floor jack, four jack stands, and a set of car ramps. The floor is concrete so I can use a mechanics creeper to roll around under the car and a mechanics stool to work on items on the side of the car. I also have electrical outlets on both walls and enough extension cords to reach all the way around the car.

I have two electric heating panels that I bought at an auction. I attached them to the garage wall and connected a thermostat to the panels to control the temperature. I also have a kerosene heater as a back-up if it gets really cold. **Safety tip:** Safety is paramount so don't create any fumes if you are heating with anything that has an open flame (like a kerosene heater). Gas, paint fumes, or cleaners can ignite and ruin the whole project (along with your shop and possibly your house)! It is also important to have good ventilation if you are using the kerosene heater. I only use mine as a back-up and to take the chill off in the shop. If it is so cold that I can't get the shop warm enough to work in, then I don't work. Even when it is cold, a good pair of coveralls and heavy socks can make a world of difference. My hands and fingers are what usually get cold enough to take a break. When you can no longer hold onto the tools, it is cold enough to stop, right?

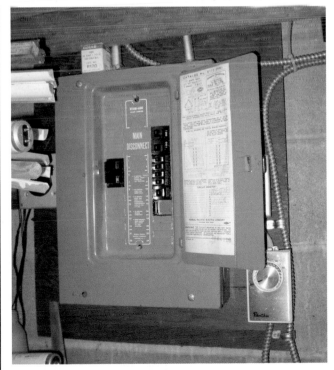

If you have the chance to have a separate shop (or even if your current garage doubles as your shop), make sure you have a separate electrical panel installed. I have 220-volt service available in my garage for things such as compressors and welders. I also don't have to worry about overloading the household circuits and making my family mad when the compressor kicks in.

CHAPTER 5
WHAT PARTS TO USE?

Now that I have a car and I have a place to work on the car, what am I going to do to the car? Before I can decide on what kind of modifications to make, I need to figure out what I can afford and what kind of capabilities I have in the shop.

All of the modifications I was considering needed to be affordable, relatively easy to install, and street drivable. Affordability to me is relative to my pocketbook and not yours. Look at your extra cash and decide how much you can afford to put into the car. Maybe you start with one project in the fall, another in the spring, another in the summer, and so on. Many people might not be able to jump into all the items at once while others can buy everything they need the same day they buy the car. In my case I wanted good quality, but reasonable prices. My goal was to get the car done without having to put it in the shop, then take it out of the shop.

In my quest to find parts I discovered a company called The Tire Rack (www.tirerack.com), which offers the "Upgrade Garage." The Upgrade Garage is an online section of the Tire Rack website that allows a user to select a vehicle make, model, and year, and to search for parts for that vehicle. You only select the model once and it is saved in your "garage." If you have several vehicles you can save them each under their own names. I entered the 2002 Honda Civic EX, my wife's 2003 Mustang convertible, and my 2007 Dodge Nitro. Once entered, I could log into my "garage" and search for different parts that were specific for the vehicle. While the Tire Rack doesn't sell everything I want, it does have a large number of parts. Most are perfect for the budget builder. Items such as suspension components, intakes, exhaust, wheels, tires, and more are available. With a couple of clicks I can see all the products they sell that are designed for my specific car.

One thing I really like about the Upgrade Garage is the tire and wheel section. A buyer never knows what the wheels look like on the car without installing them. It is pretty impractical to install a bunch of different wheels just to see what they look like before I buy them, but in my "garage" I can. I can change wheels and see what they look like on all my vehicles. Not a bad way to preview before spending the money. They also update the site pretty regularly. I had

I wanted parts to change the look of the body, but not dramatically. I also wanted parts that were complementary to the Honda Civic design. Razzi was the name that everyone kept mentioning when I asked about ground effects kits to meet those requirements. I grew up in a fiberglass factory and figured I have the ability to modify or even make the parts I wanted if I had time. But I am also inherently lazy. Lucky for me, Razzi parts also have a reputation of fitting with very little modification needed, and, as you can see, they are a subtle way of improving the Honda Civic's looks.

Above: Yes, I would like a car that was totally decked out. But, my budget and my time will not allow that. I'll have to resign to look at these types of over-the-top performance show cars at events such as the Specialty Equipment Manufacturers Association's (SEMA) annual show.

Left: Even the engine I really want will have to wait for a future car. This is an example of a total-tune-up engine compartment. I think there is more money under the hood of this car than in my completed car.

just picked up my 2007 Dodge Nitro (one of the first in my town) and the Tire Rack already had it on the site.

As far as the parts, I had originally wanted suspension, engine, body, and audio systems. After I started shopping for the parts, I needed to reevaluate what I was buying. Being on a budget limits the type of parts I buy and install. I can buy good-quality parts but I am not able to cough up enough for all of the modifications to be top-of-the-line items.

BUDGET

The budget I set was to put the car back into an average retail price range. I paid just under $5,000 for the car and it had a book value (without the salvage title) of about $10,000. That made my budget about $5,000 in parts. I didn't include labor, since I was going to be doing the work.

After talking to a couple of different shop owners, the summary was that most builders would put about the cost of the car into the modifications, doubling what the car is worth. I wanted to keep the cost down as low as possible. But that didn't mean I wanted to buy junk parts. If I could get anything used, I would. Shopping eBay and local swap meets is another way to cut a few costs. In my case, I got new parts.

Tuner parts are for sale through a number of different online shops. Check with more than one vendor. You don't have to buy all your parts from one shop, but make sure you consider shipping and handling charges. Sometimes the higher cost of the item might be offset by the freight charges. You might be better off ordering the same part in conjunction with another order, even paying more for that item, but saving on the freight.

EXTERIOR

One item I wanted to improve was the look of the car. I would have liked to repaint the whole car with some wild and crazy paint job, but decided that it was too much work and expense for this car. Besides, the paint was really good.

I opted for a ground effects package. There are many options available from a lot of companies. Did I want a wing or a spoiler? How about side panels? Front and rear dams? I couldn't make up my mind. But, when I talked to some custom painters and custom shops in the area, one name kept coming up as exceptional quality, easy fitting, and reasonable price: Razzi. I ordered front and rear, sides, and a factory-style rear deck spoiler. Razzi builds its products out of a "specially formulated AERO-FLEX thermostat, co-extruded ABS composite plastic material."

The material is a kind of flexible plastic that withstands dents and bumps, and looks like it came from the factory. When installed it doesn't have any exposed screws or rivets.

The parts fit with very little modification, slight sanding here and there, then sealing and painting. And use adhesive to attach to the car. All you need to do is fit the parts, sand the finish, and paint the parts. After the paint is dry, apply the adhesive, and then stick the parts to the car. Razzi parts are not only easy to install, but look and fit great at the same time. The paint shop was surprised at how simple they looked and how little I did to get them fitted. In fact, it's possible to install the front and rear bumper skins to the car without the adhesive, and you have a hard time believing they are not part of the bumper—the fit is that good. The running board panels fit well, but did not stay in place without the adhesive and a couple of screws. Assuming all its parts fit as good as the Honda parts we had, I would not hesitate to use Razzi again.

My original plan was to fit the parts and, if I had the time, paint them myself. If you don't own spray equipment but have a compressor, there are very reasonably priced paint guns available at the local home stores (Home Depot, Menards, and Lowe's) and many of the auto parts stores. I opted for a small, no-name, gravity-feed gun from Menards and spent less than $30 for it.

My smaller compressor was more than adequate to paint the parts. Don't tell your painter friends (or Razzi), but if you buy enough aerosol cans of paint, (the same color as the car or a contrasting color) you can actually paint the ground effects parts yourself without a compressor. I think the biggest problems in painting are having the parts prepared and a dust- and dirt-free place to spray the paint. It doesn't matter how good the paint gun or how great your sanding and preparation are if you have to paint in a driveway with the wind blowing. It's a no-win situation and you will never be able to get a satisfactory finish. Anything is possible with today's paint: aerosol, paint gun, or even brush (not recommended but I do know people who have) as long as the facility is dirt-, dust-, and bug-free. When all else fails, fit and install the parts and have them painted at a paint shop. Most of the body shops I called were more than happy to paint the parts, as long as they didn't have to spend the time to install the parts.

I also wanted a few other cosmetic touches. Besides the ground effects package, I wanted wheels and tires and vertical doors. Vertical doors are one of the neatest modifications (besides large-diameter tires) of the last few years. Vertical doors are not required but you have to admit, having a Lamborghini-style door system is pretty impressive on any car. There are numerous manufacturers offering vertical door kits. Some are weld-on, most are bolt-on, and most companies manufacture something for the Honda Civic. After talking to customizers, one of the things I discovered was

Left: Upgrade Garage is offered on the Tire Rack's website. This useful service allows people like me to preview tires and pick components that are designed specifically for our cars. This might be the only way to preview the wheels you want to buy, before you make the purchase.

Below: I have really got to get me one of these! If not the car, at least I have got to learn how to paint the realistic-looking flames that have become so popular. I wanted a fancy paint job, but my car was being built on a budget and might even spend time in a high school parking lot. I don't think I want to spend that much money on the paint.

that the vertical door kits have a habit of becoming out of adjustment and not sitting right after a short period of time. It appeared to me that the better kits have more adjustments and more mass in their construction, which also makes those higher priced. I wanted to put a good vertical door kit on this Civic; I wanted something that would adjust reasonably easily, be simple to install, and safe. After reviewing the number of different designs, I decided to spend a little bit more money on the door kit and get something that was highly recommended by one of the local shops.

Lambo Style Doors (LSD) have the best construction and most adjustments of any on the market. LSD doors also have met side-impact safety requirements in Europe. What better set of vertical doors to put on a car that will be driven

LSD makes some of the best vertical or Lamborghini-style door kits on the market. Not only do they fit well, but they allow you to open the door conventionally if you don't have the space or if the winds are too high.

When you open the LSD door kit, you will be impressed with the quality of the parts and how well it fits right out of the box. It basically comes complete with everything except wiring extensions. The kit for the 2002 Honda Civic bolted directly to the car. The swing arm needed to have the holes modified to fit our door.

by my children? Not only will they look good, but they maintain some integrity into the structure of the car. But, because of their quality they are also one of the highest-priced vertical door kits on the market. Because of the quality and safety, I decided to forego the racing seats and a few of the interior cosmetic parts and spend that money for the LSD door kits. And I'm glad I did.

Besides the ground effects kits and the Lambo Style Doors, I still wanted to improve the looks of the car with either paint or graphics. In the interest of money and time, I opted for some basic graphic kits from Sharpline graphics. Sharpline offers numerous designs and colors that can be applied by a customizer or by the owner. It is one way to get the effect of a modified-looking car without the expensive custom paint job to worry about. (I have to admit I would have liked painted-on flames on the car. If I was better with an airbrush, I was thinking this Eternal Blue Honda Civic might look good with, say, new styled flames painted in silver on the hood. But again, consistent with the goal of the book, building a cheap tuner—and the fact that I am not very good with the airbrush yet—I decided to use owner applied graphics.)

SUSPENSION

What tuner car doesn't have a suspension mod? My thought exactly. I wanted to lower the vehicle for looks and hopefully improve the handling at the same time. The perfect solution would have been a total suspension package with shocks, coils, etc. But after looking at some of the prices of the complete packages I figured the best deal might be to just add a new set of lowering coils to the existing shocks. One thing I didn't take into account originally was the fact that the original struts might be bad. In my case, the rear shocks were good, but the front struts were leaking and damaged. In the long run, I probably could've bought performance struts for not much more money than I paid for the original replacement struts. Either way, I ended up installing new struts on the front, with new lowering coils, and only replacing the springs on the rear.

WHEELS AND TIRES

I also had to take into account the types of wheels and tires that I was going to put on the car. Tire Rack had really nice packaged prices. I was able to put the Honda in the "Upgrade Garage" profile and view different wheels on the car. I had thought about 18- or 20-inch wheels, but then decided to not lower the car. I didn't want to worry about the tires and wheels being damaged too easily in turns and going over speed bumps and normal road debris. After a discussion with Matt Edmonds, the marketing guru at the Tire Rack, I settled on the Motegi DV5 wheels in a 17-inch diameter. The tires need to fit these wheels, which are 215/45/17. The DV5 wheels are a slightly twisted five-spoke wheel available in bright chrome, black, silver or Anthracite (kind of a smoke finish). I chose the Anthracite finish.

Even though I really wanted 18-inch wheels, Edmonds highly recommended that if I was to keep this a budget car, I should stick to 17-inch wheels and tires. He reminded me again of the reduced cost, less risk of damage and clearance problems, and that they look just as good as the 18-inch wheels I wanted. And really, who will notice the actual size when the car goes screaming by with the nitrous pumping?

ENGINE

As far as the engine, I originally wanted a turbo (or maybe a supercharger), nitrous, oversized pulleys, cold-air intake, header and exhaust, fancy wire covers, and other cosmetic decorations for under the hood. But sticking to the plan of budget parts, simple bolt-on installations, and ease of operation, I dropped a number of the items from my wish list. While a few items, such as the pulleys, wouldn't be that expensive, I really wanted a nitrous oxide kit. I decided to spend my money on the nitrous and skip the pulleys this time around.

It's surprising what a set of new wheels and tires can do for the appearance of a car. The Tire Rack website gave me the ability to preview the tires and wheels in the Upgrade Garage.

With the goal of increasing the horsepower as easily as we could, I researched what the starting horsepower should be. If the Honda was new, the 1.7-liter engine should generate about 127 horsepower. That's new and not abused horsepower. But let's figure this 100,000-mile engine might be a little tired. My thought is that I can conservatively estimate that I can get about 110 to 115 horsepower out of the run-in, stock engine. While it is faster than the average lawn mower, it's still not going to be a speed demon. What I need is a way to increase the horsepower as simply and cheaply as possible.

Think about what an internal combustion engine needs: Fuel, oxygen, and an ignition source to generate the combustion. If we can increase those items we should get an increase in the power that the engine puts out. Using the Nitrous Express package will help put more oxygen and fuel into the engine. Installing a better air-intake system will increase the oxygen flow to the engine. If we can cool the

47

The Honda Civic EX comes standard with a 1.7-liter, 127-horsepower engine. While it's still a VTEC engine, it's not the double overhead cam engine that's included in the SI.

air as it goes into the engine, it will contain more oxygen. It is pretty basic: increase fuel and airflow and get more power.

If we can get more fuel and air into the engine, we also need to get the burned chemical out of the engine. One way to do that is to install a less-restrictive exhaust system. Better airflow from the exhaust will come in the form of a better-designed header, smoother bends in the exhaust, and larger-diameter pipe used in the exhaust system. In this case, a good stainless header and cat back exhaust system from Performance Import Trends should pick up about 5 to 10 horsepower.

Once I took off the heat shield I realized there was already a header on the car. It appeared that when this car was rebuilt, the builders put on a few aftermarket parts and skipped factory stuff to help cut the costs. It already had a set of projection headlights and now a header. I'm assuming the guy didn't pay much money to put this header on it because it was rusted, lightweight, and in terrible condition. It needed to be replaced if for no other reason than it

was ugly. The replacement header is stainless, made of heavy walled construction, and highly polished. Not only will it do well in controlling the exhaust, it looks great under the hood without the heat shield.

Tie the new header into a 2-inch titanium exhaust system and you can't help but get an improvement in performance and power. Although, when you install the new exhaust system, the original catalytic converter and sensor remain. I increased performance before the catalytic converter and after the catalytic converter, but lost performance when the exhaust passed through the converter. I would have removed all the parts, but the goal was to keep the cost down and make this street-drivable—and street legal means leaving the catalytic converter on.

By adding the AEM Short Ram Intake system it is estimated that I can get another increase of almost seven horsepower (6.6 horsepower to be exact). With one more option I should be able to get about 200 horsepower out of this basic 1.7-liter, four-cylinder engine. Since this car had a

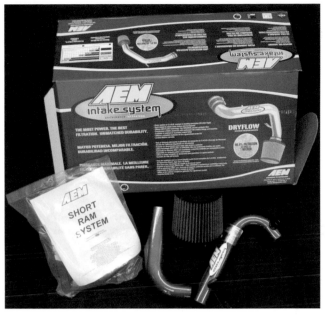

Above: Another way to improve performance is to increase the amount of air the engine can get. Getting rid of the bulky resonator box and air intake box and replacing them with an AEM short ram intake should improve our performance by about 6.6 horsepower. Plus, it looks good under the hood.

Left: One of the simplest ways to improve performance is to improve the exhaust. Performance Import Trends offers a well-built, good-looking, stainless-steel header.

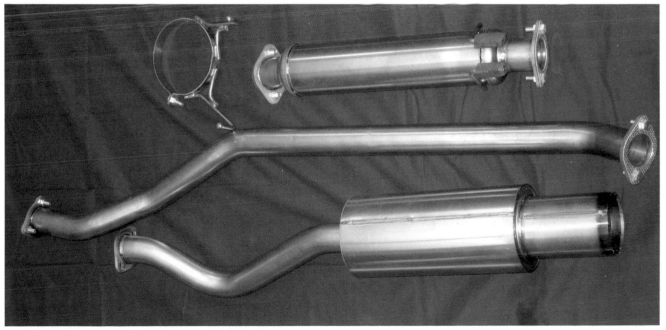

Performance Import Trend's cat back exhaust is made from titanium and is extremely lightweight and durable. Besides looking good, it should offer a tremendous improvement in the sound and add some horsepower to boot..

damaged air-intake resonator box and assorted bent and broken brackets, a new intake system was a no-brainer. What brand and model was up in the air, so I went back to the Tire Rack website, logged into the "Upgrade Garage" using my existing Honda Civic information, and started a search for different intakes. AEM was the manufacturer Tire Rack used and after looking at a few different models I opted for the Short Ram model. I also thought I would spend a few extra bucks and get the blue powder coat so it would accent the car's color.

NITROUS

That last performance option is nitrous oxide. The one neat thing about nitrous oxide is that it works very well with almost any type of engine. It doesn't matter if it's a four-cylinder, four-cycle engine or a two-cylinder, two-cycle engine, nitrous can increase the horsepower. Nitrous oxide basically acts like a supercharger. It has been called a "liquid supercharger" because of the way it reacts in the engine and increases the power like a supercharger. A supercharger mechanically forces more fuel and oxygen (air) into the cylinders, compacting and compressing the mixture. More fuel and air results in more power generated during the combustion. Nitrous does sort of the same thing.

Let me try to give you a quick summary of how nitrous works when used to boost horsepower. When you heat nitrous oxide to around 570 degrees Fahrenheit, it breaks into oxygen and nitrogen molecules. When you inject nitrous oxide into an engine it provides more oxygen to mix with the fuel. Since there is now more oxygen, more fuel can be injected at the same time. Now we have more fuel and air in the cylinder (like the mechanical compression of the supercharger), allowing the engine to produce more power. When nitrous oxide breaks into oxygen and nitrogen, the nitrogen helps reduce the heat generated by the combustion. Additionally, when nitrous oxide vaporizes it has a dramatic cooling affect on the intake air. When you reduce the temperature of the air it becomes denser, thereby providing more oxygen in the engine cylinder. Basically, nitrous oxide is one of the simplest ways to provide a big horsepower boost to any engine at a fairly reasonable cost. Whew . . . did you follow all that? Quick Cliff Notes version: We inject nitrous and we get more power. If you add a simple nitrous system you should be able to pick up anywhere from 25 to 75 horsepower. Nitrous Express offers

Since I wasn't going to do a lot of work to the interior of the car, I thought it would be good if we added a few trim pieces. Superior Dash offers a very complete carbon fiber kit that is simple to install. I ordered a dark-blue, carbon fiber package.

Above: Auto Meter Products sell a large number of instruments and gauges. Adding nitrous also requires that we watch the temperature of the nitrous, along with paying attention to the water temperature and the fuel pressure. I ordered four gauges. Auto Meter Products sells a pillar mount for two gauges and I bought individual mounts for the other two gauges.

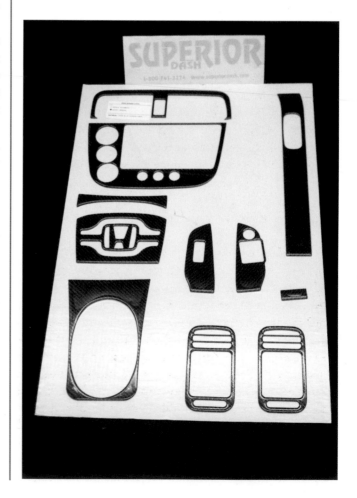

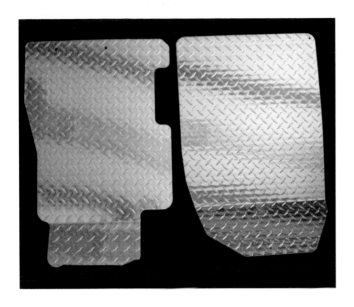 

Left: One last package I ordered was a diamond plate aluminum floorboard kit. It includes two pieces of aluminum designed to be used as floor mats, and will change the look of the interior and give it a race car appearance. Right: Nitrous Express offers a complete installation package for the do-it-yourself mechanic. It should be noted that nitrous is not expected to be used on the street. I have the basic Import single-port "Hitman" system. This package puts a nozzle in the intake and has a button/switch to inject fuel and nitrous. Make sure you read the instructions when installing.

one of the nicest and simplest systems available and they are priced very reasonably. Probably the biggest difficulty with adding nitrous is that most insurance underwriters will not insure the car with an active nitrous system.

Do not overheat the engine if you use nitrous. You'll be pumping more fuel and oxygen into the engine than normal, so make sure the cooling system is keeping up and that the nitrous oxide is at the right temperature to break up and do its job. To do that I ordered a water temperature gauge and a nitrous oxide temperature gauge. I also ordered a mount to install in the cabin of the car. Auto Meter Products makes a very high-quality, yet reasonably priced set of gauges and mounting hardware.

DISADVANTAGES TO NITROUS

But, there are problems with turbochargers, superchargers, and even nitrous oxide, the biggest of which is detonation. Detonation is an uncontrolled form of combustion that adds undue stress to the inside of your engine. Detonation occurs when excessive heat and pressure in the combustion chamber cause the air/fuel mixture to ignite from pressure and temperature, not from the spark plug. This means there are a couple of different ignition points instead of just the one spark from the plug. As these different combustions happen they will collide in the combustion chamber (cylinder) and create a sudden increase in the cylinder pressure, which is often revealed by a metallic pinging or knocking noise. The impacts created by detonation subject the internal engine

components (head gasket, piston, rings, spark plug, and rod bearings) to severe pressures and overloading.

Detonation can be controlled by the use of higher-octane fuel, and/or a combination of better fuel and retarding the timing. In our favor, most of the newer nitrous oxide systems are pretty well designed and only require a limited readjustment of timing. But it is still a problem that needs to be managed.

There is another disadvantage to a nitrous oxide system: the nitrous oxide gas. The tanks can be pretty small and a lot of nitrous is required to generate the increase in horsepower. That's one of the reasons that nitrous is that last little extra "push" of power. Push, meaning a switch or button is engaged at some point in the engine operation to give the engine a burst of power. Typically the engine needs to be operating above a certain rpm and temperature to take advantage of the nitrous and not destroy the engine prematurely.

As a side note, nitrous has been used for years to increase performance and to help dentists. Aircraft in military and racing situations have used nitrous to boost performance at higher altitudes where the air is less dense. Dentists have used nitrous as an anesthesia, often referred to as "laughing gas."

I did consider adding an electric supercharger, which most of the manufacturers claim will give me a gain horsepower increase of about 5 percent, but stopped short of buying it. I didn't want to overly tax this old engine. But it is still an option if I want to boost the power a little more.

CHAPTER 6
GENERAL PREPARATION

Now comes the best part: taking the car apart. The easiest way to work on the car was to put the whole car up on jack stands, allowing easy access to the underside of the car so I could work on the exhaust system. Also, I recommend removing the old wheels and tires so there is space in the wheel well to work on the suspension and the engine.

It's always good to start with a few basic precautions while getting the car ready to work on. Disconnect the battery and remove it from the car. Always remember to remove the black, or negative, lead first so that you don't bump something and create an arc. If you remove the battery, don't set it directly on concrete; make sure that you put a block of wood under the battery or set the battery on a shelf in a cool, dry area. Be careful not to tip the battery and spill the liquid on your skin or clothing. Make sure to clean the battery with water and baking soda before you put the battery back in the car.

Make sure you have jack stands close by, access to the tools, and someone to help you complete these initial preparations. It's also important to keep track of the parts you remove. Many parts won't be reused, like in the case of the door hinges. But a lot of the items, such as the strut bolts and the fender bolts, will need to be reused. To keep track of the bolts use Ziploc bags and a permanent marker, or plastic containers or old soup cans. Ziploc bags don't take very much room and are pretty cheap. With today's digital cameras, it might be worth your while to take pictures of the item before you disassemble it. Or, only do one side of the car at a time. It's kind of nice to be able to look at the side of the car that is still assembled to know where the parts go. If you've ever forgotten which bolt went where, you know what I'm talking about.

Jacking the car up seems to be such a simple process, but it's amazing how many times a car falls off the jack. Make sure that your jack is in good condition and clean. Any time you raise the car in the air, someone should help or watch, for safety reasons. I like to start with the front of the car because the emergency brakes are usually on the rear of the car. Once the front of the car is in the air and the jack stands are firmly in place, then you can remove the jack. Then do the back of the car. In my situation I left the jack in place after lowering it just to put pressure on the jack stands. Having the car raised in the air made it easier to access the lower fender bolts, strut bolts, and exhaust.

Ziploc bags and a permanent marker are a cheap way to keep track of parts. By labeling the bags, you won't mix up bolts with other projects.

Knowing that I was going to work on the doors and replace the strut springs, I removed the front fenders. When you remove the fenders, be careful not to break all of the plastic rivets. If you do break some, check your local auto parts store for replacements. Removing the front fenders not only gave me room to work on the door hinges and the struts, but it prevented me from scratching them when I leaned over the car to work on the engine. I put all the bolts and plastic rivets and clips from the fenders into Ziploc bags labeled "right front fender" and "left front fender." Once you install lowering springs and the larger wheels and tires, you won't have very much room between the fender and the tire. You'll need to use smooth plastic rivets or screws so as not to rub the tire, and these need to be installed prior to lowering the car.

On the Honda Civic, there is a plastic fender liner between the fender and the door that will need to be removed. The liner won't be reused once new hinges are installed for the doors.

Left: It is always safer to unhook the battery. Accidental starting, sparking, or arcing can create problems. Loosen the battery terminals with the appropriately sized combination wrench or a ratchet and socket. Remove the battery cables. Start with the negative or ground cable (black). Typically you remove the black (negative or grounding cable) first to reduce the risk of shorting the system. Right: In this case, the battery was held in place with a piece of wire. I cut the wire with a diagonal cutter (wire cutter) and removed the wire from the car. Be careful when removing the battery not to tip it sideways and spill any of the battery fluids (acid).

During the process of removing the fenders also remove the bumper. Depending on your car, you might not need to remove the bumper skin, but in my situation, the bumper skin was loose and not fitting the fender correctly, anyway.

After removing the tires and wheels, and then the fenders, I sprayed Liquid Wrench Penetrating Oil on the rusted and dirty strut bolts. (This car appears to have sat out in the salvage lot for a while.) Many of the nuts and bolts in the engine compartment were rusted and corroded. I bought a large can and sprayed all the rusted parts in the engine compartment.

Make sure that you spray the penetrating oil on the corroded bolts on the header and exhaust system. All those rusty bolts may as well be soaking while you are doing some of the other work.

To remove the bumper, it's necessary to remove the plastic rivets on top of and below the bumper.

Left: After the rivets are removed, press a small screwdriver or putty knife in between the seam of the bumper and the fender. There is a block attached to the fender that has three clips holding the bumper in place. When you depress the clips they release the bumper from the fender. *Right:* Remove the bolts that hold the bottom of the bumper in place using a wrench and a socket and ratchet. Once the bumper is unbolted and the clips are released, you can remove the bumper and set it aside.

The license plate will need to be removed and the bumper cleaned up and modified slightly before the Razzi air dam can be installed.

Left: After the bumper is removed, remove the screws that hold the bumper clip bracket in place. Two bolts are removed and the plastic bracket is set aside (in a plastic Ziploc bag labeled for the correct fender). *Right:* The fender liner has small screws toward the front of the vehicle that can be removed with a socket and ratchet, or you can use a nut driver.

Left: Under the light is a bolt that holds the light and fender in place and another bolt that holds just the fender on. Remove both bolts so that the front edge of the fender can be removed. *Inset:* The plastic rivets holding the liner to the upper side of the wheel well were easily pulled loose using a diagonal cutter. Grip the center of the rivet and pull the rivet out. Yes, it does usually ruin the rivet, so make sure you have purchased a box of replacement plastic rivets before you put the fenders back on the car. Most of the rivets can be replaced using 5/16-inch plastic rivets.

Left: Using a nut driver, socket, and ratchet, or even a combination wrench, you can remove the bolts that are located on the top of the fender. The bolts attach the fender to the frame and will be used to adjust the gap of the fender (to the hood and door). *Middle:* The forward bolt is located next to a smaller screw that holds the headlight assembly in to the fender bracket. When you remove this screw, make sure that you keep track of the expansion nut that is installed in the fender bracket so it does not get lost. *Right:* Using a 10mm socket, remove the two bolts that attach the fender bracket and the headlight assembly to the vehicle.

After removing all the bolts from the top of the fender (don't forget the one bolt behind the front edge of the door), remove the fender and set aside. The fender will need to be modified prior to reinstalling so that the LSD door hinges will clear.

Above: I started the rest of the projects by jacking the front of the car. I blocked the rear wheels and also applied the emergency brake. I wanted as much height as possible so I also placed a small section of a 2x4 on the jack to give me a little more distance. After the jack was extended to its maximum, I placed two jack stands under the frame. I then lowered the jack so that the frame (and the weight of the car) was resting on the jack stands. Cars fall off of jacks. Never climb under the car without first placing the jack stands securely. A safety reminder: The jack can be used to lift the car, but it should never be the only support.

Left: The jack stand needs to be placed under an area of the frame that will not move (such as a swing arm or suspension component) and was big enough to sit securely on the jack stand saddles. Two of my jack stands are of the pin type and two are the ratchet (or locking pawl and tooth version). Whichever type of jack stand you use, make sure the locking mechanism is secure before removing the jack. When you release the jack, do it slowly until the weight has settled onto the jack stands. Make sure the vehicle is sitting securely and level before attempting to raise the rear of the car.

CHAPTER 7
INTAKE INSTALLATION

You can start wherever you want to, but my first step was to squeeze out a little more horsepower from the engine. The first thing I did was remove the intake resonator box, brackets, and associated parts. My car was a salvage car and the air box and the mounting brackets actually had damage. It all needed to be replaced. What better way to replace it than with an AEM ram, short intake? Having the intake removed gives you a chance to look at the rest of the engine.

In my case, electrical box brackets were broken, the intake resonator box was broken, a few other brackets were bent, and a few items were repaired. Even the housing that the upper radiator hose attaches to had been re-welded. I knew the car had been wrecked, I had just hoped for better repairs. Overall it was fixed pretty well. During the test drive and inspection I noticed nothing really unusual in the way it handled.

It is always a good idea to review the installation instructions before you start the work. How many of you have the attitude that I can do this and "I don't need no stinkin' instructions?" That's always my first thought. But please review each product's instruction before you get started. It makes things go a lot smoother. Take my word for it. I'll admit, that's experience from this car talking.

The intake installs very easily with little or no problems. The intake does incorporate the original air sensor unit and in our case includes a modification for the nitrous nozzle. I installed the intake first and got everything connected and mounted prior to drilling any holes for the nitrous. Make sure that the nitrous nozzle is installed in a location that's easily accessible and that the stainless lines from the solenoids can reach the nozzle. For that reason, install the intake but *do not* modify it for the nitrous just yet. Another reason for doing this relates to whether your car is an everyday driver. If you are driving the car, you can make this modification in about 30 minutes and be back on the road with an increase in performance. It is that easy.

As I mentioned before, the intake system on this car had a few problems. The resonator box actually had a couple of holes that were unrepaired. I suppose these allow more air flow and could improve the performance.

Not only was the resonator box damaged, but so were the mounts. The mounts on the box were cracked or broken and the mounts in the car were bent.

Note the damaged leg of the resonator box. This would have been important to fix if I hadn't already planned to change the intake system.

Above: Remove the bolts that are in any of the mounts on the air box or resonator. Even if the mount is broken, remove the bolts. The new intake system only uses one of the intake mounts, and the rest just get in the way. *Left:* Remove the resonator box and mounts. I disposed of the unit since mine was damaged.

Using a 1/4-inch drive socket, extension, and ratchet, remove the bolts on the air filter cover. What happens to the parts is up to you. I put all the parts in a box to be thrown away at a later time. If you think you want to put the old intake system back on (I don't know why you would), keep the parts for later.

Once you have the air filter cover removed, lift out the air filter. You will have better access to the breather hose, brackets, and sensor.

Left: A view of the air filter box, filter removed

Below: To remove the breather tube, all you need to do is squeeze the wire clamp with your fingers or a pair of pliers. Loosen the clamp and slide it toward the engine and off the hose. If it is too tight to move, use a screwdriver to help move the clamp off the hose.

The breather tube may be stuck to the metal tube. You can break the seal with a screwdriver pushed under the lip of the hose. Once the tube is unstuck you can twist it by hand and remove the tube from the engine breather.

After removing the breather hose clamp and loosening the hose from the tube, remove the sensor connection and lift the air filter housing from the engine. Make sure that you do not lose the sensor unit in the air box; it will be reinstalled into the AEM intake systems. As you can tell, I left the filter in the housing in this photo for no good reason. Carefully remove the air sensor and set aside. The sensor unit just slides out of the housing. It is reinstalled in the AEM intake after the intake is installed.

After the air box is removed, you have full access to the intake and throttle body.

Above: The new AEM intake will not use the old rubber connector on the throttle body so remove it and place with your collection of extra parts.

Right: Using a 3/8-inch drive ratchet and 10-inch extension, I removed the extra resonator housing bracket. I was hoping to possibly use this for the nitrous solenoid brackets but decided its location would not be appropriate.

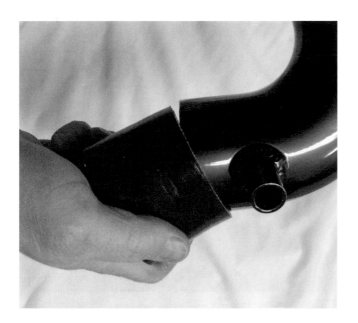

Left: Attach the smaller coupling hose to the long end (end that mounts on throttle body) of the intake. Make sure the coupler is far enough on the intake to be securely fastened under the hose clamp. Install as far as possible until it almost touches the breather tube. *Right:* Compress the sensor grommet that is provided by AEM and insert it into the provided opening. The grommet needs to be inserted completely so that the inner lip is completely inside the intake pipe. If the grommet is not completely installed, the sensor cannot be installed. The sensor grommet completely installed in the intake should look like this.

Left: Slide the worm gear clamp over the coupler tube and slightly tighten it in place. You will not want to tighten the clamp completely. If you have enough pressure to hold the clamp and coupler in place, you can adjust the location of the worm gear so that you can access and tighten the clamp once it is installed on the throttle body of the engine. *Right:* If you start the coupler at an angle and slowly twist the assembly, the coupler hose will slide over the throttle body. Don't forget to put the other clamp on the coupler before you start the assembly. If you do, like in this picture, you will get the intake installed and have to remove it to install the clamp. After the intake and couplers are in place, tighten the clamps. Don't over-tighten and damage the clamp or pinch the coupler, but tighten it enough to keep the intake and coupler from moving. This is where you will turn the clamps to offer the best accessibility to the worm gear screw. Align the screw so that you have unobstructed (or at least as unobstructed as possible) access.

CHAPTER 8
HEADER INSTALLATION

Once I was done with the intake system, I started on the header. The biggest problem I ran into on this car was the corroded nuts and bolts. Two of the top header bolts also hold the stainless heat shield in place. I removed those bolts and then tried to remove the lower heat-shield bolt. It wouldn't budge. I tried Liquid Wrench, an air ratchet, and a breaker bar. The nuts were so corroded that it finally started to slip in the sockets. I even reverted to a pair of Vice-Grips with no luck. Since I was changing the header and didn't plan to install the heat shield I decided to use a long pry bar and pry the heat shield away from the bolt. My intent was to tear the rusted shield. Yes, I basically ruined it, but I did get it off the header.

After removing the heat shield I was able to remove the remaining three bolts from the header with a socket, ratchet, and extension. All of the bolts were removed very easily and I dropped them in to a magnetic tray to hold them until I was done. I might have forgotten to mention the magnetic tray. I bought a small dish-shaped one from Craftsman. The tray has a magnet in the base that holds it to a metal part of the car and as I remove bolts I drop them into the tray and they don't roll under the car. It also holds sockets, wrenches and other items until I need them. This is not a replacement for the Ziploc bags. If I started on the header and was not going to get the work done fairly quickly, I would move the bolts to a labeled bag. But in many situations, the bolts are going right back on the car, so I want them accessible in the magnetic tray.

Removing the catalytic converter from the header required using an impact wrench. These bolts were rusted and the penetrating oil helped. They could have been removed with a ratchet, socket, and extension. If possible, replace these bolts with new bolts—it makes for a cleaner-looking installation, but it's not required. Typically I wire-brush the bolts and inspect the threads to make sure they are not damaged before I reuse them. If the threads or heads of the bolts are damaged, they are replaced. Most of the kits I installed included new nuts and bolts.

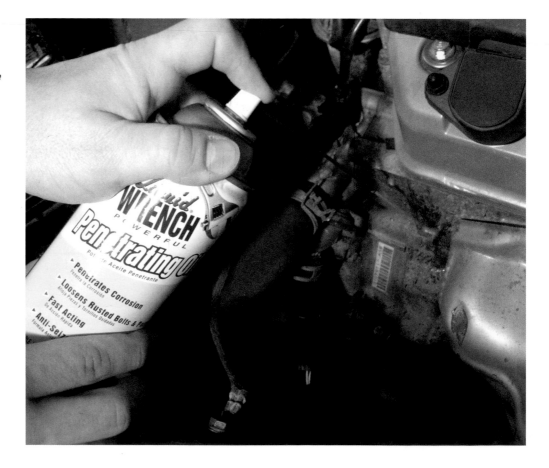

Liquid Wrench is a staple in a shop that works with rusted bolts. Spray the penetrating oil on all of the header bolts that are visible. After the removal of the heat shield, access to the rest of the bolts will be possible.

Remove the heat shield bolts. These are also the top two bolts that hold the header in place. If they are too tight to use a ratchet, you could use a breaker bar or impact wrench, but be warned that the bolts or studs could break off in the head—a bad thing. More penetrating oil and time would be a better solution than a bigger wrench.

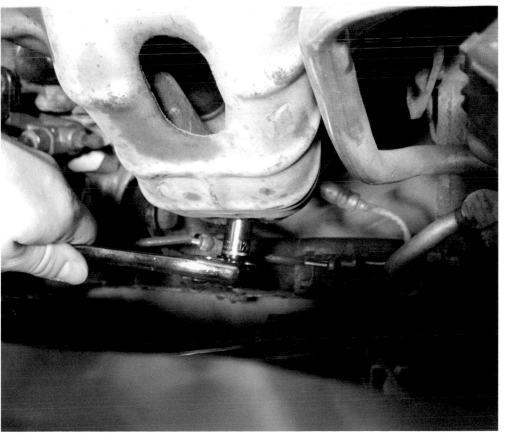

The lowest bolt on the heat shield bolts into the exhaust manifold. This bolt was corroded and rusted so badly that the head of the bolt was breaking up. The socket and wrench didn't work; neither did a pair of Vice-Grips. I finally had to use a pry bar to pry the heat shield away from the bolt, causing the shield to tear. I know, not the best mechanical thing to do, but I was ready for the shield to be off. I wasn't planning to reuse it anyway. And even if I did, I could have used a large washer to cover the torn spot.

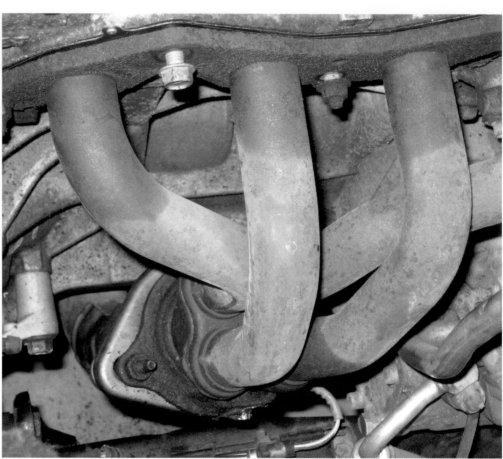

Above: *See, even after the shield was removed it didn't look that bad. There was a small tear that we could cover if needed with a washer.*

Right: *Surprise. This engine already had a header installed. I guess the guy who rebuilt the car found a cheap replacement for the factory manifold. Did I mention cheap? This header was rusted, lightweight, and thin in a few spots. Good thing I had planned on changing it anyway.*

With a 3/8-inch ratchet, socket, and a medium length extension I was able to loosen the remainder of the header bolts. The driver's side bottom bolt was rusted and the stud actually unscrewed instead of the nut only. No problem, but the best solution is to replace the stud. The rest of the header bolts and nuts were removed without a problem. Remember the magnetic tray you bought to store nuts and bolts? Now is the time to use it. I placed the bolts and nuts in the tray to keep them handy when I reinstalled the new header.

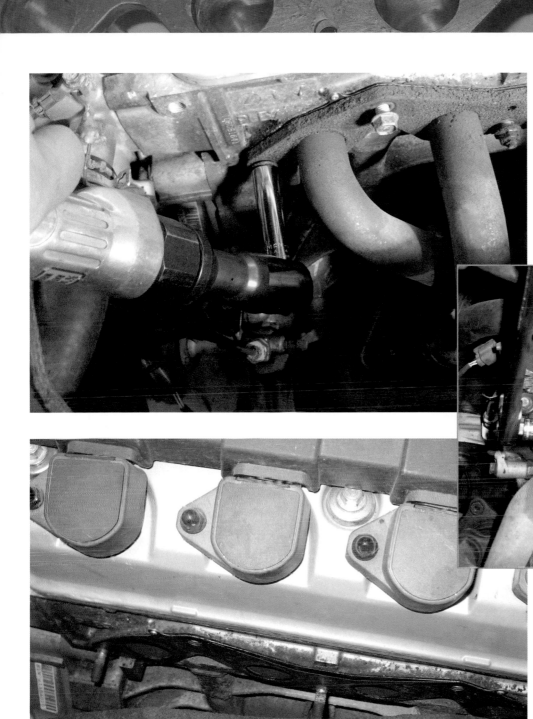

Left: You could use an air ratchet if you have one available. It speeds up the process if you have the access.

Below: The nuts on the passenger's side were removed without an extension. Since the studs were pretty long, I used a deep socket for the clearance.

Left: Once all the bolts and nuts were removed, I was able to remove the old header, carefully, so as not to damage the metal exhaust gasket. I was hoping to reuse the gasket, if possible.

Just a quick visual comparison of the old and the new header. Besides the new header's shiny appearance, the size of the material used was substantially different. Even though stainless ("it stains less") can still rust, it should have a longer life than the old mild steel header that is being removed.

Left: *Once you have the header removed, inspect the manifold for cracks, chips, or damage in preparation for cleaning the surface.* **Right:** *Clean the manifold surface with a solvent such as acetone and remove any grease or grime.*

Since I planned on using the old exhaust manifold gasket, I needed to put an application of K-W Copper Coat gasket compound on the header.

A completely coated header. After you've applied Copper Coat to the header, set the header aside so it can start to dry and get tacky.

Like the header, put a good coating of the Copper Coat on all of the surfaces that the gasket will contact and let the Copper Coat get tacky.

Carefully place that exhaust gasket over the studs in the engine and press it against the coating of Copper Coat. The tacky Copper Coat should hold the gasket in place while you install the header.

Once the gasket is in place, carefully install the header onto the studs making sure the gasket stays in place. Press the header firmly onto the gasket and hold the header there. While you hold the header in place, install the nuts and the header bolts into the engine head. Tighten the bolts and nuts by hand, trying to maintain even pressure on the header.

Once the bolts and nuts are finger tight, use the appropriate socket and ratchet to tighten the header in place. Don't over-tighten. Make sure that you rotate around the header and tighten each nut or bolt. Do not tighten just one bolt all the way. This could warp or bend the header. Tighten each bolt a little bit at a time and move to an opposite bolt. Moving around the header throughout the process will help uniformly tighten the header against the engine.

The result is a good-looking Performance Import Trends stainless-steel header. This complete job only took about 30 minutes.

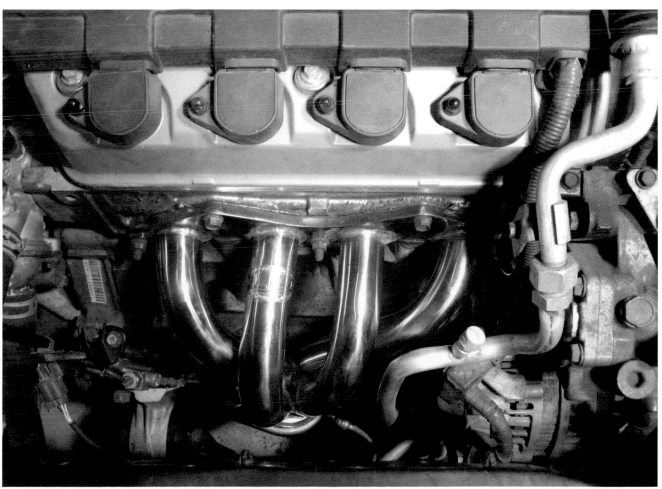

CHAPTER 9
INSTALLING EXHAUST

The next practical step is to install the new titanium Performance Import Trends cat back exhaust system. The cat back exhaust system is a lightweight titanium package. The installation process is very easy. The goal of a new exhaust system is to improve the exhaust flow and therefore increase the horsepower and of course, change the way the car sounds. There are many exhaust options available, many of which are not titanium. The Performance Import Trends cat back exhaust is exceptionally well-built, lightweight, and remarkably easy to install. The biggest problem I ran into was the rusted bolts on the end of the catalytic converter. A good soaking of the bolts with the penetrating spray helped me to remove the nuts without a problem, though they were pretty corroded so I did buy replacement nuts to use for the reinstall. I didn't replace the bolts from the catalytic converter, and I also used the same bolts that attached the catalytic converter to the header. The catalytic converter needed to be removed from the header prior to changing the header.

With the new cat back exhaust, you do not need to add a header. The cat back system attaches from the catalytic converter back. It replaces the muffler and tailpipe but doesn't affect the catalytic system sensor. It is approved in most states.

From a performance standpoint, it would've been nice to get rid of the catalytic converter and increase the diameter pipe from the header all the way back to the cat back exhaust. But to maintain the street-legal status of the car, it is necessary to keep the catalytic converter intact.

A few tips about exhaust system installations. If you spray silicone spray on rubber hangers it helps release them, and allows you to slide the metal hangers past the catches. It's also important to reinstall the exhaust system making sure nothing rubs or touches the underside of the car. The new tailpipe will be quite a bit larger than the old one so make sure that it doesn't touch the bumper and the bumper doesn't get too hot.

When you get ready to install the new exhaust, make sure that you install the large tailpipe hanger on the tailpipe first. It's too difficult to slide the tailpipe through the hanger if the hangers are installed on the car.

Left: As you look up from the bottom of the car, you'll notice the bolts are spring-loaded to maintain pressure on the header bracket. The springs also allow the engine to move in the motor mounts without stressing the joint. *Right:* Using an impact wrench was about the easiest way to remove the header bolts. Once the bolts were removed, the catalytic converter pipe could be lowered.

As you look down at the catalytic converter, you will notice it drops down away from the header but not out of the car. After the bolts are removed, the header needs to separate from the catalytic converter pipe in order to replace it.

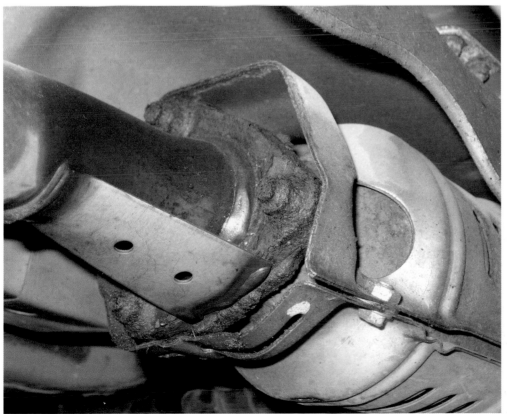

Take a good look at these corroded nuts. The only way I was able to remove the nuts was by applying Liquid Wrench and using the impact wrench with a deep socket. After removing the nuts it was necessary to wire brush the bolts to clean the threads. After the impact wrench loosened the nuts I was able use a ratchet and deep socket to finish the job.

Once the nuts were removed, the extension pipe separated from the catalytic converter. Basically the old exhaust consisted of three parts: the down pipe that includes the catalytic converter, the extension pipe or B-pipe with the resonator and the muffler and the tailpipe. The new cat back exhaust is three parts: the B-pipe, a straight through muffler, and the tailpipe.

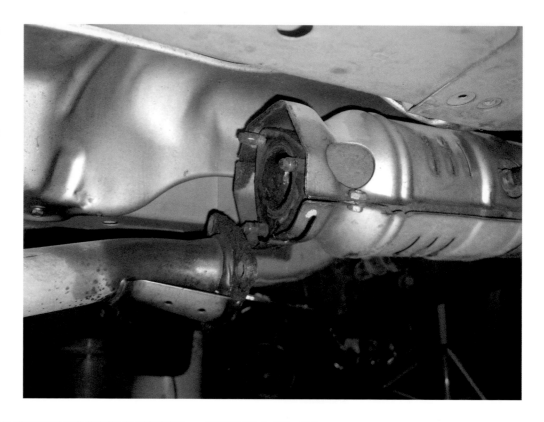

Left: Penetrating spray and a ratchet and socket was all that was needed to remove the muffler pipe bolts. Spraying the hangers with silicone (or WD-40) helped to get the rusted pins loose from the hanger's rubber grommets.

Above: If you look close you can see the new muffler going into its location and the metal hangers being inserted into the rubber hanger. This can be done before you attach the B-pipe to the catalytic converter, as we did, or after the B-pipe is installed.

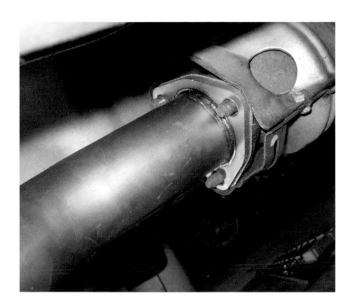

Left: The front of the B pipe is being attached to the rear of the catalytic converter. This is the only flange in the system with three bolts. The original bolts are being reused, but the new exhaust came with new gaskets, and I bought new nuts to replace the damaged old nuts. Once the B-pipe is attached to the catalytic converter, make sure that it is aligned approximately with the rest of the systems. There are no hangers on the B-pipe. Once the muffler is attached to the rear of the pipe, the pipe will be supported. Until then you will need to support it until the nuts are started. Remember, I already installed the muffler hangers. **Right:** I installed the new nuts on the catalytic converter just finger-tight to hold the B-pipe in place until I attached the muffler.

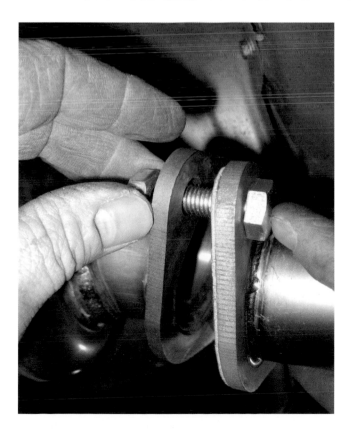

Left: Now is the time to attach the straight-through muffler to the B-pipe. By supporting the rear of the muffler with the hangers, you can just pivot the muffler in position to connect it to the B-pipe flange. Install the included bolts and gasket, and tighten. **Right:** Tighten the bolts while making sure the rest of the exhaust system is not touching any of the underside of the vehicle.

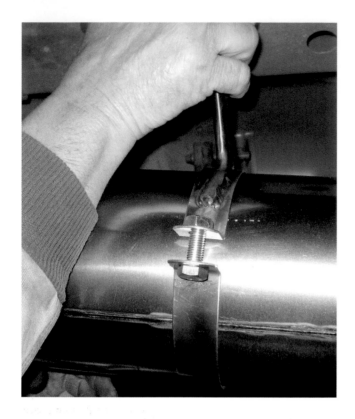

Left: Loosen the clamp and slide the tailpipe hanger over the pipe. Leave the clamp loose until the rest of the connections are completed. *Right:* Slide the tailpipe hangers into the rubber grommets. Again, silicone spray or WD-40 will help the hangers go through the rubber holes.

Left: After installing the hangers, connect the front of the tailpipe to the rear of the straight-through muffler. Use the new bolts, nuts, and gasket provided. By installing the hangers first, it allows you to pivot the tailpipe and align the flanges of the tailpipe and muffler together. Finger-tighten the bolts making sure there is clearance all around the pipes, mufflers, and tailpipes. After you are comfortable with the position, tighten the nuts and bolts with a couple of wrenches or a wrench and socket and ratchet. *Right:* The new tailpipe looks huge! Make sure the bumper skin does not contact the tailpipe or you could burn the plastic. This total job only takes about an hour. This is another quick solution that improves the sound and performance of your car.

CHAPTER 10
INSTALLING FRONT STRUTS

I would have really liked to change the suspension to a complete coil-over package with adjustable shocks and struts, but the budget wouldn't allow it. So the next best thing was a quality set of lowering springs.

My goal was to lower the vehicle without reducing the ride, and to make the car look more like a performance machine, rather than a stock Honda. Just by changing the front and rear springs you can change the appearance and the handling of the car. Lowering springs need to be a little stiffer to keep the car from bottoming out on the bumps, and stiff enough to reduce body roll in the turns. The ST lowering springs are "developed for daily driving and feature moderate lowering for a sporty look and improved handling, without sacrificing ride quality"—exactly what I was looking for in springs.

For a low-cost modification, the ST Suspension Sport Springs will lower the center of gravity, which in turn should reduce the body roll in corners and limit the weight transfer under acceleration. I am very happy with the way the car looks, handles, and rides, despite lowering the car and stiffening it up.

Installing the springs was a very simple job. Although it actually cost me more than just springs, I had to buy struts. Once I started removing the old struts on the front, I noticed how bad they were leaking and that the rods were actually damaged. Replacement struts cost about $140 each. This was an expense I hadn't really planned for. When I made my inspection of the car it didn't appear that the struts were damaged or leaking. I decided that if I was this far into the car, why not spend the money and put the new struts on. I am glad I did.

Changing the struts and springs (front and rear) was going to require a spring compressor. This is one of only two tools I had to borrow. I could have bought one, as they are pretty reasonable.

I was really glad to have an impact wrench when changing the struts, too. The bolts were very difficult to remove with hand tools. I have a small air impact that runs off my compressor, but it was unable to loosen the bottom bolts on the front or rear. I borrowed an electric impact that had more power to get the job done. In most cases my air impact works, but it was not able to handle the large-diameter bolts that were corroded and stuck in the bottom of the shocks and struts.

The original struts and spring are ready to be removed. If you look closely you can see the stains from the leaking struts.

On the Honda Civic EX there are two bolts that hold the lower portion of the struts to the swing arm. Both those bolts needed to be removed before we can remove the strut. Use a 1/2-inch drive ratchet and socket along with an impact wrench (with an impact socket) to loosen the nuts and bolts. At this point, just remove the nuts.

This is another instance where you can use the impact wrench or a ratchet and socket. It's surprising how easy it can be with an impact wrench and how spoiled you can get using it. Slowly compress the spring until the pressure is reduced and you can move or turn the cap.

Above: These bolts could be pretty tight; you might have to pry on them with a pry bar or use the ratchet to turn them out a little to start the removal. The lower bolts should (once loosened and with the spring compressor taking the pressure off the springs and struts) slide right out of the brackets.

Left: Once you have the nuts removed and are confident that the spring compressor will not slip, remove the bottom bolts from the strut.

Left: Slowly and carefully lower the struts out of the tower and away from the control arm and set it aside.

Above: You'll find alignment marks on the strut cap and on the spring retainer. You will want to mark those with chalk or a marker so that when you reassemble the strut and the spring it will be aligned correctly.

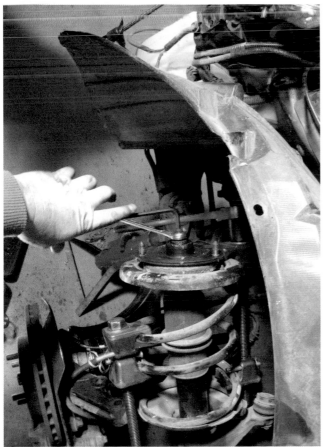

Left: To remove the strut cover you will need a hex wrench for the shaft (center of the strut) and an open or box end of a metric combination wrench for the strut nut. Hold the hex wrench firmly to keep the strut shaft from turning while using the combination wrench to loosen the nut. This will also relieve the cap from the spring pressure. Do not remove the nut until the spring pressure is completely released. Make sure the nut is still on the shaft with a couple of full turns. With the nut firmly on the shaft, release the pressure on the spring compressors evenly and in small increments until the cap is loose and the nut can be removed without fear of the springs pushing on the cap.

Above: If you are unable to hold the hex wrench firmly, as was my case, put an old jack handle over the long end of the hex wrench to add leverage.

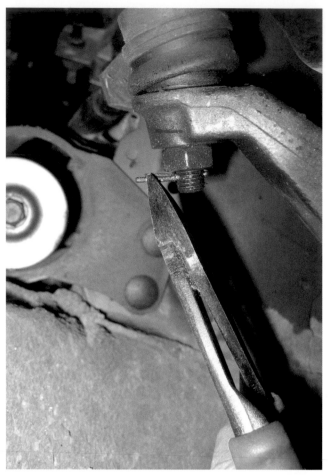

This is what the strut assembly looked like just before removing the nut and taking off the cap and the spring.

Right and below: New struts require removing the tie rod from the strut control arm. First you must remove the cotter pin in the ball-joint nut. After removing the cotter pin, remove the nut from the ball joint bolt. For this I could use a ratchet and socket or even the impact wrench.

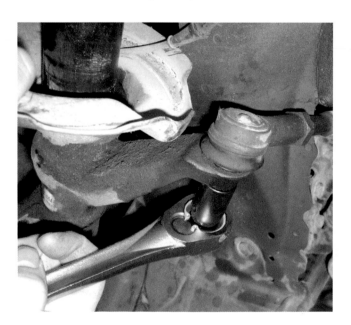

Right: The tie rod/ball joint tool, or "pickle fork" as it is often called, is probably not something everyone should or would own. But it is the only thing that will really do this job. The pickle fork wedge end is driven between the ball joint and the control arm with the intent of forcing the ball joint out of the taper in the control arm. Sometimes this happens very easily and sometimes it takes a small sledgehammer to get the job done. In my case, the small sledgehammer was necessary. Once separated, the strut assembly can be removed from under the car and put in a location to make changing the spring easier.

Left: The new ST front lowering springs. Note the tighter coils on one end compared to the other. The lighter end goes to the top, per the instructions.
Right: Comparing the old spring with the new spring you will notice how tight the coils are. It is interesting to note that this is a lowering spring and we should drop about 1 inch, yet the new spring is about the same height overall as the original.

Left: If you look close you can see the damage to the strut. *Right:* The damage and the leakage was the deciding factor in replacing the strut assembly with new struts. I could have saved about $300 by not putting on new struts, but it was going to be necessary in the very near future anyway. Just as well do it now—I would hate to have to go through all of this work again.

The new struts looked great. Even though I was able to find struts on short notice, I was unable to get any of the other hardware. That meant I needed to use the old boot, caps, retainers, and nuts.

Below left: The strut boots are an easy install; if you want it to work better, spray the shaft of the strut with silicone and the boot will slide right into place.

Below right: Note the location of the spring end and where it is to be located on the strut spring base. There should be a bump or indentation to hold the spring and help keep it from twisting once installed.

Make sure the spring retainer cap aligns correctly with the end of the spring, and with the alignment marks that were located earlier.

Below left: Place the strut cap on the spring cap and align the marks. With the lowering springs we were able to assemble the strut and springs without using the spring compressor. Firm pressure on the cap allowed us to start the nut on the strut. It takes an extra set of hands to hold the assembly while the nut is tightened. The hex wrench is again used, and if necessary an extension on the hex wrench, to hold the shaft while the nut is tightened. With the combination wrench, tighten the nut until it has stopped at the bottom of the threads on the strut shaft.

Below right: Replace the strut into the tower and start the three nuts finger-tight. Do not tighten completely at this time.

CHAPTER 11
INSTALLING REAR SHOCKS AND SPRINGS

The rear spring installation is really just a continuation of putting the springs on the front. The ST package includes springs for the front and the rear. Again, the ultimate goal of changing springs is to reduce the center of gravity and improve the handling, and, of course, the looks.

The top of the rear shocks was accessible through two access panels behind the rear seat. Remove the plastic panels to see the top of the shock and the two bolts that hold the top into the frame.

One bolt was accessible from inside the trunk without any extensions. In this case, we were able to use an air ratchet to remove the bolts.

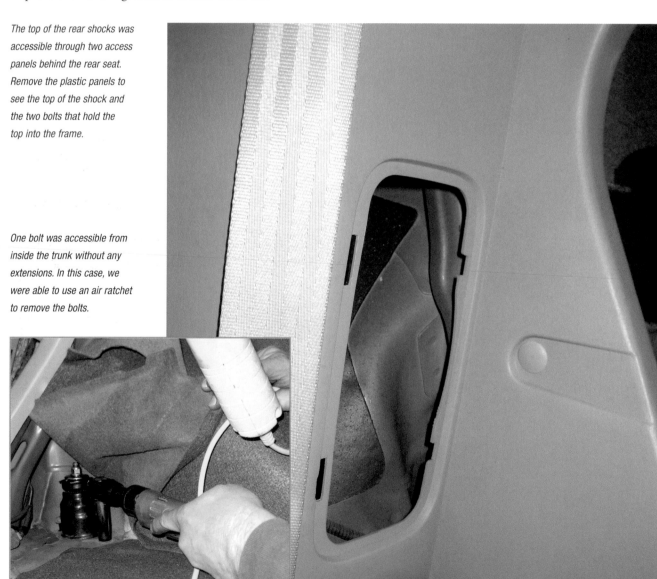

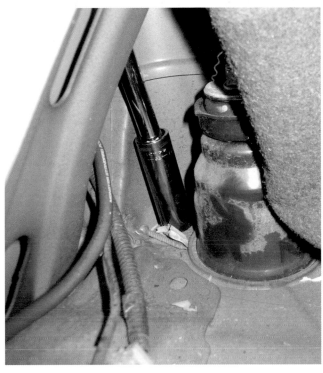

The outside bolt was a little more difficult to reach. I folded the rear seat backs down and removed the bolt with a ratchet and socket using a 10-inch extension.

Above: *After both bolts are loose, remove the nuts and go to work on the lower bolt.* **Right:** *Before you remove the lower bolts it will be necessary to compress the rear springs. The area to work in is very small and with the large spring compressor you might only be able to compress one side. Since these are smaller springs, compressing only one side should be sufficient if the compressor has a very good attachment point. If you have a smaller or different compressor, by all means, use it on both sides of the spring.*

Above: Spray the bolt nut and the housing with Liquid Wrench to help loosen the bolts and make the removal easier. Remove the nut and bolt.

Right: After the bolts are removed, slide the shock and spring assembly out of the mounts and start the disassembly. Like the front struts, there is a nut at the top of the shock that needs to be loosened slowly. The shaft of the strut is again held in place with the hex wrench and the nut loosened. Once the nut is loose, slowly loosen the spring compressors. After the spring compressors are removed and the spring retainer cap is moving freely, remove the nut.

Make sure you know where all the parts go. The rear shocks did not get replaced. All of the old parts—except the springs—were being reused. Any damaged parts need to be replaced. Dirty parts should be cleaned before reassembly.

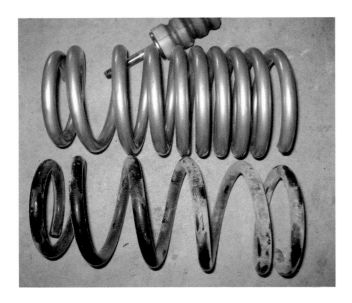

New and old springs. Like the front, the coils are tighter, yet about the same size. Make sure that you follow the instructions an out the tapered end of the coil toward the top.

Install the new springs on the old shocks, locating the ends of the springs in the indentations. Replace the boot, washer, and caps in the same order as they were removed. A digital picture is a great resource.

Left: Lift the assembly into position and have someone start the nuts on the top bolts. Finger-tighten the top bolts until the rest of the assembly is installed. Once all the bolts are in place, tighten the bolts on the bottom swingarm and then the top bolts. Replace the access panels behind the seats. Right: Assembled and ready to use. Once the car comes off the jack, the difference in height is noticeable if you paid attention to the car before the change. Our car dropped about 1/2 to 3/4 inch in the rear and about 1 inch in the front.

CHAPTER 12
INSTALLING DOORS

Many people feel that the vertical doors and large-diameter wheels are two of the biggest parts of the auto customizer's market. I agree. I think vertical doors push a custom car one step above other custom cars. Almost everyone I talked to warned me about putting on the vertical doors, saying they are a tremendous amount of work. I was also told that the car needs to be modified and that I would have to weld things in place to make the doors work correctly. For me, none of those comments were accurate. Maybe it's because I used LSD doors, or it might be because those people just didn't know what they were talking about. I think both.

But there are disadvantages. Vertical doors require more alignment and adjustments than stock doors. Some vertical doors require welding to the pillar. Other doors claim bolt-on-only but require constant adjustments and lots of modifications just to get the doors to work.

On the positive side, LSD doors are one of the only types that have had safety testing done for side impact—a major issue for me. Plus, LSD door kits have numerous adjustments available to make sure the doors fit and work properly. Their product is also built with substantial mass that seems to keep it within adjustment a lot better. LSD doors can be opened conventionally to about 25 to 30 degrees without ever having to lift the door vertically. I can get in and out of the car without worrying about lifting the door if it's windy or raining or I am in a parking garage that has a low ceiling.

*Left: First unhook the door stop. **Right:** Next, unhook the rubber wire covers from the doors and trace the wiring harness to the plugs inside the car.*

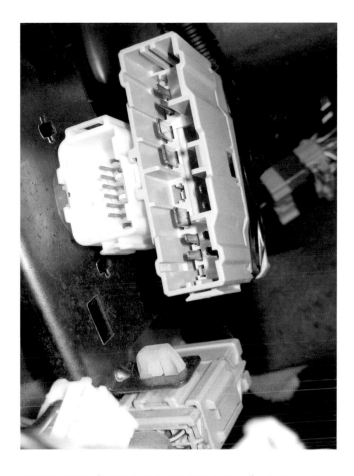

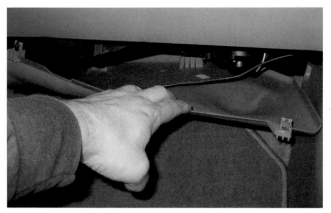

On the passenger's side, loosen the panel at the bottom of the dash to access the plugs. Again there are two plugs, but both should be about the same size. You might be able to access the plugs from behind the glove box of your car. As you look under the dash on the passenger's side, you will see the two plugs side by side. Use a screwdriver to release the clip and unplug the wiring loom.

This looks hard to do, but it is really easy. Push down on the clip and unplug the wire looms. There should be two plugs on the driver's door of the Civic EX. One is a pretty large plug and the other is smaller. You will need to lie on your back and look up toward the door pillar to see the plugs

It's amazing how easily the doors operate. Once they were adjusted, which only took about 10 minutes, we were able to open and shut the doors one-handed with no effort in or out of the car. Operation was very important because my daughter and wife would be using the car.

One disadvantage to putting on vertical doors is wiring the loom. The easiest way is to cut all the wires and solder in extensions, heat shrinking the whole mess of wires together. This car has power door locks, windows, etc. There were probably 30 wires that needed to be cut and extended. You could cut and extend the wires by purchasing some additional pigtails and creating an extension. Easier said than done! The Honda dealer near me, which was mentioned before, was not very helpful and was unable to find the pigtails or plugs that I needed. But, I was able to find my own pigtails on wrecked cars at a place called Wrench N Go in the local area. Wrench N Go is one of those places where you go to its lot, remove the part you want, and pay when you leave. I am actually really

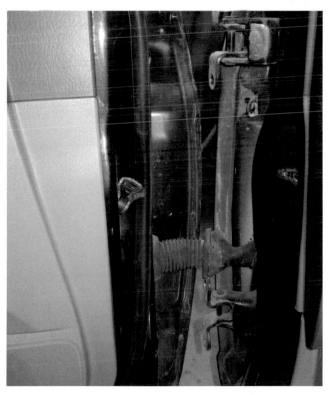

Pull the wires out of the car through the access hole in the side of the hinge mount. Unbolt the doors from the hinge using a socket and ratchet. For safety's sake, you will need an additional person to hold the door so that it does not twist and bind the bolts or fall. You could always use a stool or blocks to support the door while you remove the bolts, but be very careful. If the door twists and/or drops it will scratch and dent the door, or worse, pinch or scratch you. Another tip: Work on one door at a time; that way one door is still in place if you need to see how something fits.

The door plate is bolted on.

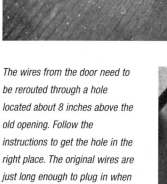

Left and above: Just when you thought it was safe to bolt the doors on . . . a minor adjustment was needed. The swingarms that attached to the door of the Honda Civic were off about 1/4 inch so the holes needed to be modified. To do that I used a die grinder and a carbide tip. The air die grinder was the perfect way to enlarge the mounting holes in the swing arm. I suppose it could be done with a Dremel tool or by hand with a file, but it would take a while. I enlarged all four holes just over 1/8 inch. Make sure you wear safety glasses and gloves, as the little shards of metal from the grinder fly everywhere.

The wires from the door need to be rerouted through a hole located about 8 inches above the old opening. Follow the instructions to get the hole in the right place. The original wires are just long enough to plug in when the door is down. The loom needs to be extended.

Above, right and below: Once the swingarm holes have been modified, install the swingarm to the door with the supplied bolts and Loctite the threads.

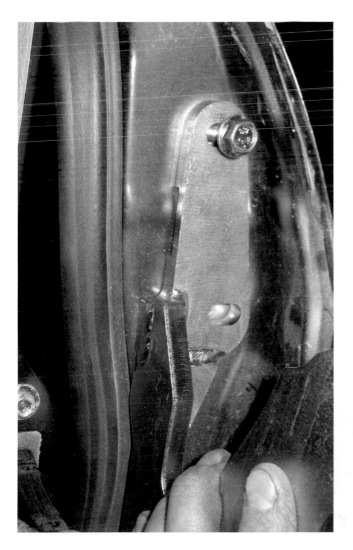

With the swingarm installed on the door, place the swing arm mount into the correct location on the plate to start the four hex-head bolts. Make sure to use Loctite.

Above: Once the four bolts are started, carefully shut the door so that it latches in place. Make sure the wires are not in the way of the swingarm or plate. Tighten the mounting block.

Right: The door is now mounted to the plate. The gas strut is not connected and the adjustments have not been made.

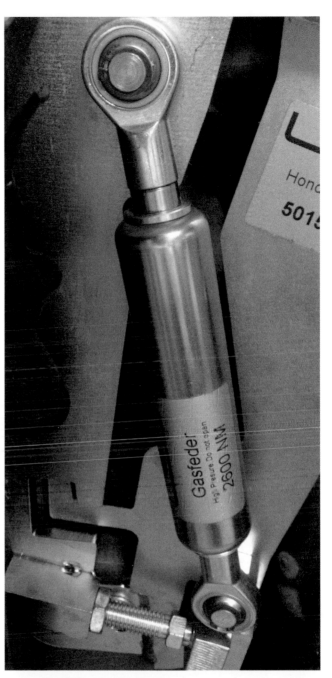

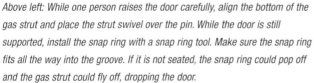

Above left: While one person raises the door carefully, align the bottom of the gas strut and place the strut swivel over the pin. While the door is still supported, install the snap ring with a snap ring tool. Make sure the snap ring fits all the way into the groove. If it is not seated, the snap ring could pop off and the gas strut could fly off, dropping the door.

Above right: Once the snap ring is installed, lower the door and again carefully shut the door until it latches. Make sure that nothing is binding or in the way during this operation.

Right: At the bottom of the swing arm is a ball-headed bolt. This bolt needs to align with the cup. The cup can be moved in and out to align the bottom of the door. This ball bolt helps hold the bottom of the door up and adjusts the door gap at the bottom. It also is the adjustment for the doors striker assembly. Adjust the bolt out until the door shuts and locks properly. You can tell if it is not out far enough by opening the door; if the door seems to drop down after it is past, the lock the bolt needs to be additionally extended.

The finished installation of the door hinge.

Below left: After the door is adjusted and all the bolts are tightened, there is one last bushing that needs to be installed. This is a spacer located at the front of the plate that helps keep the plate assembly from twisting. When the door is up, there is a lot of leverage on the door plate, so don't forget this additional support. My kit was sent without the compression nut. (Compression nuts are nuts that fit in a hole, and as you tighten the bolt the nut expands to lock it in place.) We had to drill a hole and feed a nut to the back side of the location and insert the bolt.

Below right: Using a flexible finger we were able to grasp the nut and feed it into the frame of the car through an existing access hole.

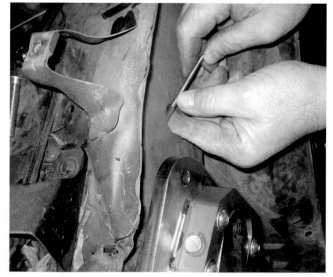

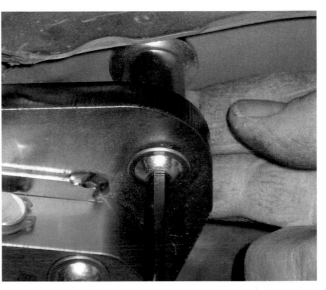

Left: With one person holding the nut in place, the other person placed the bushing behind the plate and inserted the bolt, slowly turning the bolt until it started tightening up the self-locking nut. *Right:* This bolt was tightened and the flexible finger was removed.

The nice thing about LSD doors is the ability to open them normally and still be able to get in and out of the car.

Below: Raising the doors is a very easy, one handed operation. The gas struts almost lift the doors by themselves.

Right: When the doors are lifted all the way up, the gas struts hold them in place.

Left: Closing is the same simple process. The gas struts support the doors and make the closing process a one-handed event.

Below: With the doors completely open you can see the hinge plate and swingarm. All we have left is just one adjustment.

Left: There is a small set screw installed at the front of the swingarm hinge. The set screw is turned in or out to set the stop when the door is opening conventionally. This set screw controls the angel the door opens. In our case, the bracket controlled the angle and the set screw was not needed as a stop. *Right:* If you need to adjust the stop, use a hex wrench to turn the screw one way or the other.

Left: The adjustment made allows the door to clear the roller as seen in this view. *Right:* When the fender was removed, this piece of plastic liner was between the fender and the door post. It will not be reused. The LSD door hinge takes up all the room for the liner.

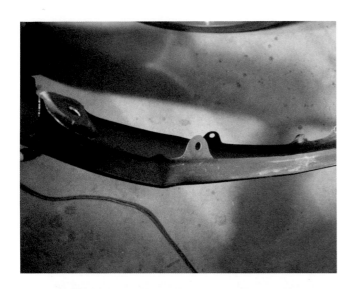

Above left: Since we are not using the liner, we are also going to have to remove the tabs that hold the liner. Additionally, the inside lip of the fender needs to be trimmed, removing the tabs and making room for the LSD hinge and swing arm.

Above right: A good pair of tin snips can be used to remove the excess fender material just below the tabs and the groove. The fender is actually pretty lightweight and it doesn't take too much effort to remove the metal.

Left: Snips will leave a few jagged edges (so will any other method), which need to be smoothed down. A 4-inch grinder comes in really handy if you have one. If not, use a die grinder, cordless drill with a grinding pad, or even a hand file to do the job. Any sharp, jagged edges can catch the swingarm and possibly the wiring, so remove it all.

Right: I made small relief cuts about every 2 inches. I wanted to flatten the area with a rubber mallet and I didn't want to change the shape of the fender curve if at all possible.

Below: We used a couple of extra floor mats on the work bench to pad the outside edge of the fender. A rubber mallet was used to hammer the edge (the area we had already cut reliefs in) down. The mats allowed the metal to flex slightly, yet the bench was firm enough to bend the metal. The carpeted floor mats also prevent the work bench from scratching the fender's finish. Be very careful in this process. If you hammer too hard you will leave dents in the fender. If you put the fender on a hard surface without any padding or flex, the fender will get flat spots. There is another option to flattening the metal: just cut more of the metal off. The more you remove the less strength you have in the fender curve.

Fit the fender and make sure that you haven't changed the curve too much by the modifications. Be careful; you can push and bend the fender small amounts but if you push too hard you can kink or dent the fender. The fender should be bolted at the top and the bottom during this process. It needs to bolt in place so it cannot move, just like it was permanently installed. The doors need to be opened and raised to make sure that the swingarm and the gas cylinder clear the fender.

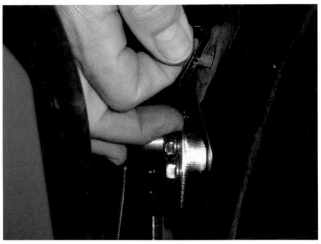

Left: Don't forget to install the bolt at the bottom of the fender under the door hinge post. If the fender doesn't want to fit tightly against the running board area, you can always add a sheet metal screw. This is important when we get ready to install the Razzi side panels. The fender has to fit snugly. *Right:* The top bolt behind the front edge of the door needs to be installed and tightened. This bolt will also control the gap at the top of the fender with the windshield trim.

On the Civic there is a plastic clip that is bolted to the fender and the inner frame rails. This assembly has small clips on the top edge that the bumper skin attaches to.

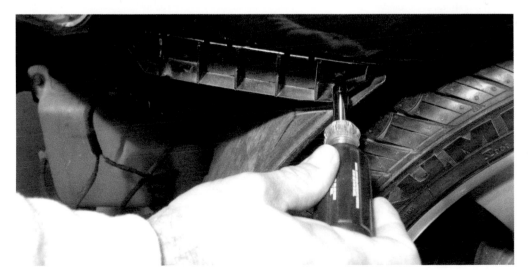

Install the bumper clip to the fender and frame. Of course, you should still have the screws and they should all be stored in the Ziploc bags marked "front fender, driver side," right?

Left: The front edge of the fender fits under the headlight bracket. There are two different bolts, one that goes through just the fender to the frame rail and the other through the headlight assembly through the fender and the frame. *Right:* There is one bolt on the top front of the fender that holds the fender in place. Use this to help adjust the fender-to-hood gap. Just in front of this bolt (under the black plastic tab in the picture) is a small plastic blind nut for a screw. The screw goes through the hole in the black tab and holds the headlight assembly in place.

Left: Once the fender is aligned, tighten all the screws and bolts holding it in place, then insert the bolt through the headlight assembly. After all this the headlights will need to be aligned. *Right:* The bumper fits in between the fender and the clip that was installed previously. The bumper needs to be pushed firmly in place until the clips catch the slots in the bumper.

Left: Note the gap or the difference in the fender and the bumper before it has been pushed and clipped in place. *Right:* The headlight assembly was loosened while installing the fenders; make sure that you tighten all the bolts.

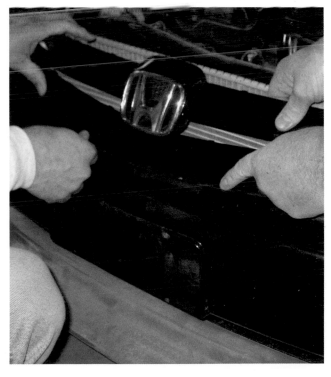

Left: Once the bumper has been installed, reattach the grill. The grill was loose when I bought the car—the reason being that it was never installed correctly. The bottom of the grill has slots that fit over pins in the bumper. Once the pins are in place, the top of the grill is attached with two screws. The screws were in a location that the bottom was not held tight. *Right:* Make sure the pins on the bottom of the grill are in place.

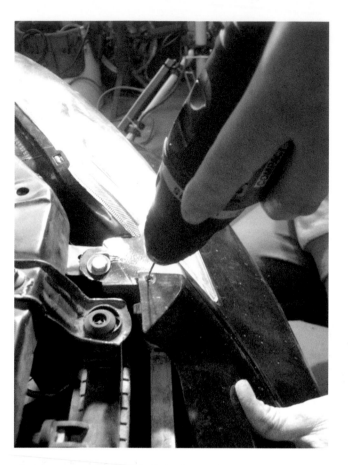

The screw locations needed to be redrilled to hold the grill firmly in place.

Once drilled, the grill was screwed into place.

INSTALLING DOORS

Left: Tighten the top bumper attachment bolts. And bolt the splash guard on the bottom of the bumper back into place. **Right:** Make a final inspection of the door and fender gaps to make sure nothing has changed. Open and close the doors carefully to check clearance and adjustments. Then enjoy the looks you get in parking lots. People would never believe how easy this really is.

CHAPTER 13
INSTALLING WHEELS

As I stated before, doors and wheels seem to be the big thing lately in customization. The diameter of wheels has gotten almost ridiculous. At the SEMA show there was a display with a 32-inch wheel. Wow . . . that's what I would have had on my F250 Ford truck. I wanted larger-diameter wheels for the Civic, but I realized there was a limit to practicality.

The Honda already had 15-inch wheels. Back in the day, we thought 15-inch wheels were big, but now 20- and 22-inch-diameter wheels are the norm, and sometimes the smaller size on some models. Even manufacturers are jumping on board with larger-diameter wheels. The new Dodge Nitro has 16-inch wheels as standard on the SLT model; 17-inch is standard on the SXT, and the performance version R/T has 20s.

A 22 would have been neat to have on the Honda, but there wasn't enough room, especially since I was already lowering the car. I started shopping for 18-inch wheels, but with the help of the Upgrade Garage and Tire Rack's Matt Edmonds, I settled on the 17s. You have to remember that even though the wheels are bigger, the tires are lower profile and often the overall diameter of the wheel and tire combination is not very different from the original package.

The Tire Rack offers complete tire and wheel packages shipped directly to your door. By using the Upgrade Garage section of www.tirerack.com. I was able to see what the wheels would look like on the Honda Civic. And when they show up at your door they are individually wrapped, mounted, balanced, and ready to install.

Assuming the car is already on the jack stands, removing the old wheels and tires is nothing more than using the impact wrench and correct-size socket. If you do not have an impact wrench, the tire needs to be locked in place using the brakes. You will need to have help holding the brakes or you will need to lower the car and put the car's weight back on the tires to get the lug nuts loose.

SUBARU OUTBACK AS A TUNER?

I have 18-inch wheels on my Subaru Outback (yes, I know what you are saying, "On an Outback?") and it looks very nice. The car is white on the top, with grey lower panels and polished black wheels. I looked into new wheels and tires because the original wheels kept corroding around the bead and the tires developed slow leaks. Each tire had been removed at least once and the bead cleaned and sealed and the tire remounted. It still didn't stop. Subaru recommended new rims. New factory rims were more than $250 each. Used, if I could find good ones, were $125 each. For that kind of money I could replace all four wheels and tires, which I did.

I think it helped the looks, but I can say this, the ride is stiffer, the new low-profile tires reduced the cushion, and they are not as good in bad weather. Most people would take them off over the winter, but we went the year without hardly any snow. When it did snow, however, the fat, low-profile tires were not very good for traction. Make a mental note to keep the old wheels and tires and put them on if you live in a snowy area.

Right: The new wheels and tires were shipped with the lug nuts and a special lug nut adapter. This looks like a stepped socket to help install the new lug nuts.

Below right: Just slide the lug nut adapter onto the lug nuts and tighten away. Use a 1- or 2-inch drive ratchet or an impact wrench. I like to install the wheel lug nuts by hand so that I don't over-tighten them or damage the finish on the lug nuts. If I have a flat and need to remove the wheels by the side of the road, I hate to have them too tight, which an impact wrench can easily do. If you alternate tightening the lug nuts (move to the nut across from the one you just tightened) around the wheel, putting equal pressure on the different lug nuts, your wheel should be installed evenly.

Above: After the wheels are tight to where you can't move the wrench, lower the car and give it one more try after the weight is on the wheels.

Left: The installed wheel and tire combination.

115

CHAPTER 14
INSTALLING RAZZI GROUND EFFECTS

Why Razzi? I wanted to make a small statement that this car was not a normal Honda Civic. Due to working on a budget, there was no way I was going to be able to put all kinds of carbon fiber body panels on the car. I also wanted to keep the paint work to a minimum. Overall, the paint on the car was good. (Although once I had the Razzi parts painted, I think they looked better than the car.)

Razzi has a reputation of ground effects packages that are good quality, reasonably priced, and, the real key, easy to install. They are not a complete replacement of any of the parts; they are what I would almost call a "snap on" cover. I don't want to imply that they are not well-attached; indeed the fit of the parts is really amazing. The front and rear dams fit the bumper without any modifications to the Razzi parts. I have installed different parts to cars and often I am grinding and shaping the parts just to get them to fit in place. Not in this case. The Razzi parts are shaped so well that all we needed to do was make the cutouts as stated in the instructions and snap the parts over the bumpers. Once in place, I made sure the cutouts were correct—they were—

and took the parts off and delivered them to the paint shop. Installation of the Razzi front air dam requires modifying the bumper slightly, creating air vents for the disc brakes. I found that putting the bumper on a work stand was easier than cutting the holes on the car. You might find it different in your situation. I didn't remove the rear bumper skin and was able to make the minor modifications required while it was still on the car.

On reinstallation, the parts fit right back into place and can be attached in a matter of minutes. Okay, so it takes longer than a few minutes but that's only because you have to take the time to put the adhesive on the panels. Once the adhesive is in place (little peanut-sized amounts spaced along the edges), put the panels back on, and let the glue dry.

The rocker panels took a little more time, but that was because we had to use a couple more sheet metal screws to hold the panels in place. If you follow the instructions, the parts can be fitted and installed in a few hours. You'll be waiting longer for the paint to dry than it takes to install the parts.

A permanent marker comes in handy to mark the areas that need to be removed. The original bumper needs to have a cutout that's about 9 inches by 4 inches because the Razzi front dam has brake vents. The bumper needs to be modified so the vent fits and the airflow can actually be used for the brakes.

Top: No real reason to do that but to prove that we didn't need any instruction manual.

Middle: There are a lot of ways to cut the bumper material—instructions say you can use a razor knife, and you can, but it's hard work. I recommend a jigsaw, reciprocating saw, or, in my case, a cut-out saw. Dewalt makes a cut-out tool with bits that work on drywall, which also work on the plastic bumper. If you have a Dremel tool, corded or cordless, you can buy a cut-out adapter and bits. It works the same and actually might be a little easier to use if it was cordless and less powerful.

Bottom: Using a drywall saw can be dangerous. The blade moves at a very high rpm and can get away from the operator, cutting bigger holes than planned. Make sure you have a firm grip on the tool and that the bumper is mounted firmly in place. We removed the bumper and placed it on a bench, but you could actually make these cutouts with the bumper still on the car. It was discovered that the cutout was easier to make if the tool was held about 1/2 inch or more above the bumper. Resting the surface guide on the bumper offered less control during the cut and the bit wandered more.

*Left: If you look into the brake vent you will notice that the freehand cut was not big enough. The area needed was misleading. We didn't cut enough and the vent was bending on the edge. **Right:** The area needed for the brake vents is actually quite large. Save yourself the headaches of cutting, fitting, and recutting—which can happen numerous times—by using the Razzi instructions and using the measurements they recommend. When we used the instructions on the opposite vent, it worked. Don't forget to "measure twice and cut once." The air dam fit without another cut.*

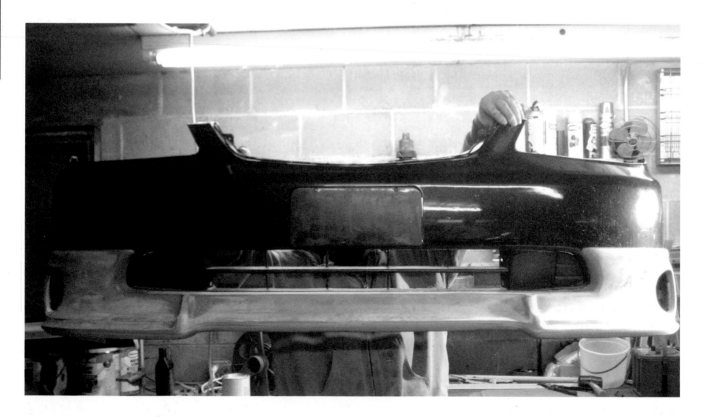

Once the openings are cut in the bumper, the Razzi air dam is slipped over the bumper and the lips are snapped around the back edges of the bumper and the wheel well edges. After paint, the Razzi dam will be put back on this bumper, with spots of adhesive on the top edge and two screws in the edge to keep it from moving. How much easier can it get?

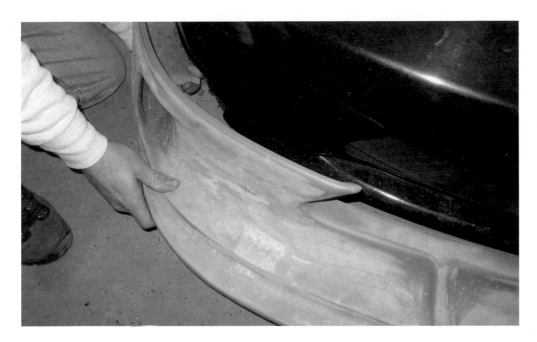

After the bumper was reinstalled, we fit the Razzi air dam to see how it looked on the car. It just "snapped" in place. Just pull the edge of the Razzi air dam around the fender and bumper and it stays in place.

It fits. I like it. Even with the lowered springs, there is still decent clearance. The Razzi components really add shape and look better than a lot of material that will get in the way of speed bumps.

The same cut-out process was required for the rear bumper. No guessing on this; we followed the instructions, made the measurements, marked the area, and cut out the bumper. This time the bumper stayed on the car. The Razzi rear dam has cutouts for dual exhaust. If your car has only single exhaust, Razzi offers a fake exhaust tip. In our case, we used the Performance Import Trends cat back exhaust and just left the cutout unfilled. You still need to make the clearance cutout in the old bumper.

Left: Measure twice, cut once, and slip the rear bumper dam in place. Sure enough, it fit perfectly without any modification. *Right:* The wheel well edge gets a couple of sheet metal screws during the final assembly.

The tailpipe from the PIT cat back exhaust fit just fine in the Razzi bumper.

The side panels did not need any modifications or cutouts. Once painted, they will be attached to the running board area and sheet metal screws will help hold them in place. Hold the panels firmly in place and install the screws. You will only need one screw in the wheel well.

I had two spoiler options. Performance Import Trends offers a carbon fiber universal wing that I really wanted to use. But that was when I really wanted to add a carbon fiber hood. Since that didn't happen I decided not to use the wing. Instead, I went with the factory-styled wing that goes with the Razzi kit. This is a fiberglass wing that attaches to the trunk lid. It comes with all the attachment hardware, including a third light and wiring.

Back from the paint shop, all that is needed is to apply small amounts of adhesive around the top edge of the front air dam.

Above: And "snap" it in place.

Right: Once the bumper is in place, two small sheet metal screws are installed to help hold the dam to the fender well area.

The finished installation.

Left: It's basically the same process for the rear dam. Remove the coating from the double-sided tape and apply the adhesive from the tube

Below: "Snap" the rear dam into place. Make sure the exhaust cutout clears the exhaust. Small sheet metal screws are installed in the wheel well area.

123

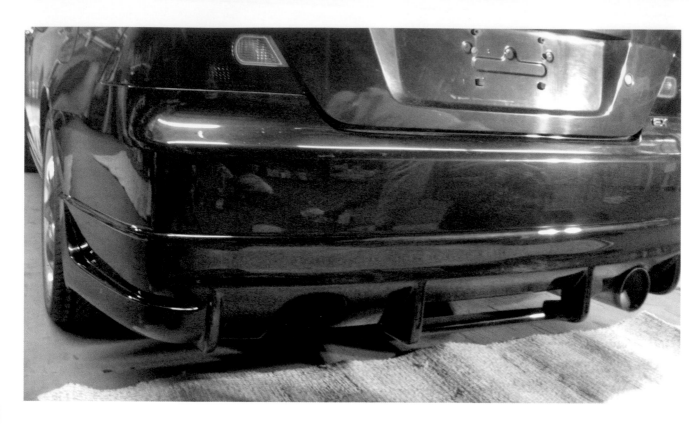

The finished rear install.

Above and opposite top: The side panels take a little more work. Before installing the adhesive, make sure they still fit and the screw holes line up. Note how well the Razzi parts fit. Little modification was needed.

Above: To mount the rear spoiler, Razzi includes what they call EZ Locator strips. These strips are inserted in the spoiler's mounting holes. The spoiler is placed in the location desired on the vehicle deck lid and the EZ Locator strips are taped in position. After they are securely taped, the spoiler is removed. There are small holes in the EZ Locator strips. Use a small drill bit and drill a pilot hole through the deck lid. Remove the EZ Locator strips and enlarge the holes for the mounting bolts. *Left:* The spoiler has a third taillight and the wires need to be fed down the inside to the passenger's side.

After the wires are completed inserted into the spoiler, attach the light with the two included screws.

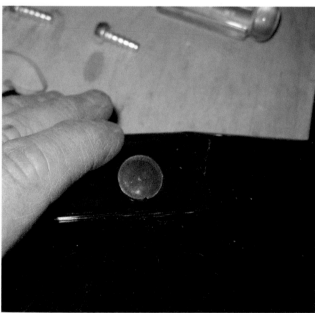

Above: Make sure the light screws are tight. After the light is secure, insert the screw covers.

Right: With the flexible finger, reach into the large hole at the end of the spoiler base and pull the light wires out. You only need the end for now. Loop the end back into one of the extra holes or tape it to the spoiler so it doesn't fall back in.

126

Insert the pins of the EZ Locator strips into the two screw holes. Do this on both ends of the spoilers. Place the spoiler in its location on the trunk lid. You can locate it wherever you want, but I placed it as far back as possible, keeping the spoiler edge about even with the trunk lid's rear edge. Make a few measurements from the rear of the lid and the side of the lid to get to correct location. Hold the spoiler in place firmly.

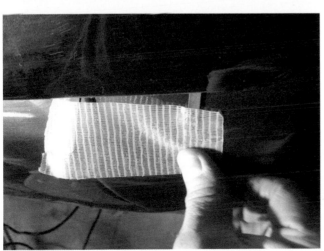

This can really use an extra set of hands to make sure the spoiler doesn't move. Tape the EZ Locator strips to the trunk lid and the rear fenders of the car. Make sure the car is clean and the tape sticks. These strips will help you drill the holes in proper places for the mounting screws. You can use masking tape or, as we did, clear duct tape. Once the EZ Locator strips are taped in place, use a flat screwdriver and slowly lift the spoiler away from the pins that are in the screw holes. This helps to reduce the movement of the locator tapes.

After the spoiler is removed, check to make sure the tape is secure and the strips do not move. I took a few extra measurements just to make sure the holes look like they are in the right places.

Using a 1/16-inch bit, drill a small pilot hole through the center of the EZ Locator strip.

After the pilot holes are drilled, enlarge the holes to the correct size to allow the screws to fit.

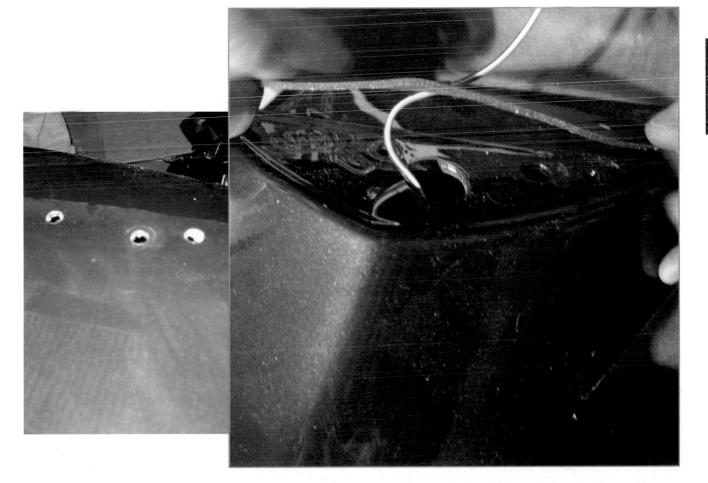

Left: Note where the third light wires exit the base of the spoiler and drill a third hole on the passenger side the same size as the screw holes. Right: Remove the protective coating and stick the foam pad to the spoiler.

Insert the screw through the deck lid and into the spoiler and tighten with a hex head wrench. Start all four screws and tighten them evenly.

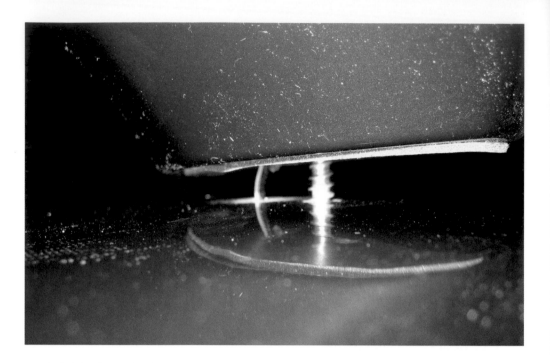

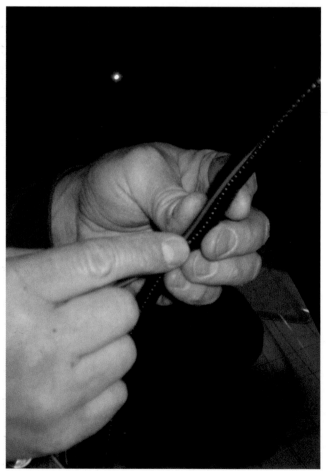

Left: Tighten all the screws so the spoiler starts to compress the foam pad but doesn't squeeze it completely. *Right:* Install the wire cover over the third light wires and run it down to the rear lights of the car. The carpet will have to be unhooked and pulled forward to get at the lights and wires.

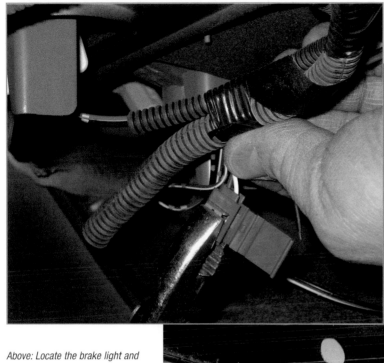

Above: Locate the brake light and the ground wire. I used a small electrical meter and located the brake light wire, which was white, and the ground wire, which was black. Connect the red wire to the power wire with the splice nut and the black wire to the black wires. Before you put the carpet back in place, check the brake lights to make sure they work.

Left: Razzi includes wire ties. Use the ties and run the wire adjacent to the other wires. Make sure the wire is not sagging or loose so that it catches in the hinge of the trunk lid. Put the carpet back in place and you're done.

CHAPTER 15
INSTALLING NITROUS

I tried to explain the advantages of nitrous earlier in the book. Increasing performance the easy way was the biggest one. But installation can be a hassle. You have to install a tank, run the lines, and manage how the nitrous and fuel are fed into the system.

Maybe now is the time to mention a few other items. This is my disclaimer. Nitrous kits are sold for off-road use only. They are not designed to be used in street cars. So, really, if you want to increase the horsepower and run the car on the street, you should probably look into a turbo or supercharger or a bigger engine. This is not an installation for street use.

In fact, if I install a working nitrous system, I think my insurance is null and void. For show, as an inoperative nitrous system, it's okay. But street use or racing, look out—no insurance.

Let me clarify again that this installation is only for show when the system is not filled and operating. When it is filled and operating it can only be used off road. Everyone clear on that?

The nitrous tank comes with two tank clamps that need to be firmly mounted somewhere. I opted for the trunk area. On the driver's side are two small plastic-headed screws that are used for cargo net tie-downs. They are just about in the right place. I used those two screws for one hole in each of the clamps.

*Left: The heads of the screws were just a little too big in diameter to clear the clamp, so I ground them down. If you want to use a bolt, that's okay; the kit comes with all the hardware. You could also use a couple of hex-head lag screws. **Right:** Drop a bolt in the existing screw hole to hold the clamp. Mark the second hole for the clamp, making sure that there is nothing below the car that you will damage when you drill through the floor.*

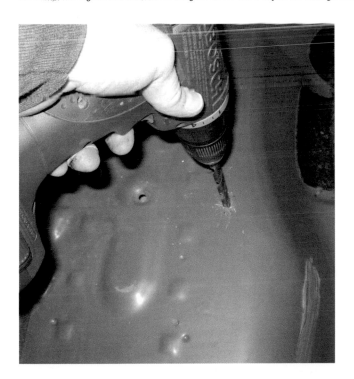
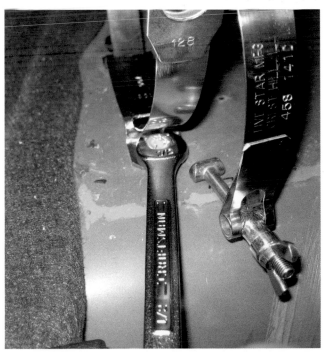

*Left: Drill the second clamp holes with a cordless drill and a 3/8-inch bit. **Right:** Install the tank clamps using the cargo screw and the included 3/8-inch bolts, nuts, and lock washers. Make sure that the tank mounts are in the correct position. One holds the tank higher than the other. Make sure the taller mount is toward the front of the car, as the instructions tell you to point the valve of the bottle toward the front of the car. Tighten the bolts and nuts with the combination wrench. Someone will have to be under the car to reach the nuts.*

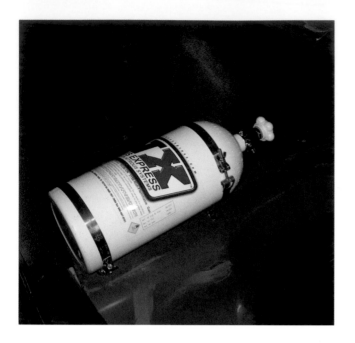

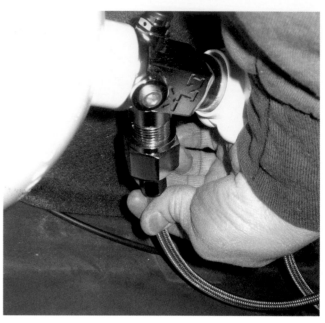

*Left: Place the bottle in the clamps and tighten the clamps. Make sure the clamps are in a secure location and do not slip off the ends of the bottle. If you drill your own holes and don't use the existing holes, move the clamps a little closer together and more toward the middle of the bottle. **Right**: Connect one end of the nitrous feed line to the bottle, just finger tight, and put a piece of tape over the other end to keep any material from getting into the line. This line is long enough to reach to the front of the car. Initially, I wanted to run the line through the cockpit of the car, under the carpet but that was turning out to be more difficult than I planned. Outside was the easiest path.*

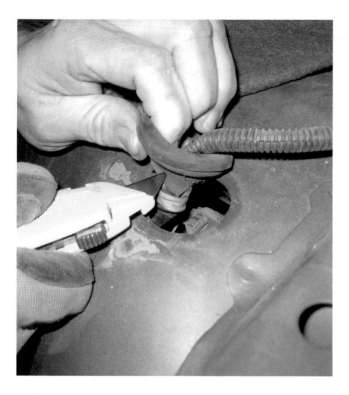

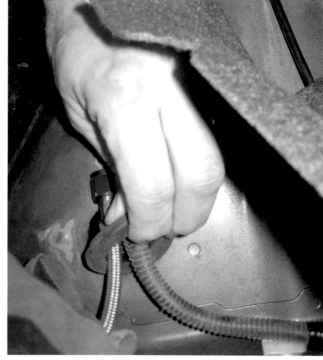

*Left: In the trunk and near the nitrous bottle was a rubber grommet that was used to seal an opening where wires passed from the inside of the car to underneath the car. I enlarged the center of the grommet with a razor knife so the nitrous line could pass through the grommet. **Right**: Feed the tape-covered end of the nitrous line down through the grommet.*

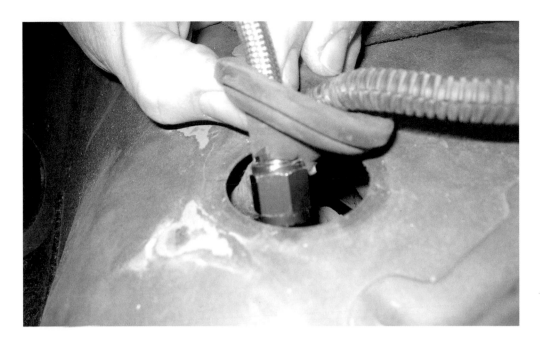

Left: Replace the grommet in the opening, making sure the "lips" are in place.

Below: To run the lines along the bottom of the car required that I jack up the car for room. This job could have been done without the jack, but it was a lot easier with extra clearance. I placed the jack and a short block of wood under the side of the car near the door sill and raised the car.

Right: Remember: don't rely on the jack. Always use jack stands, which I did at the front and the rear of the car. In addition, I left the jack in place. Make sure the passenger-side wheels are both blocked so the car cannot roll.

Below: The nitrous line exited the trunk near the fuel tank. Making sure that it would not rub any moving parts, I routed it along the tank. The instructions from Nitrous Express are pretty thorough. They recommend wire ties as a simple and efficient method of holding the line.

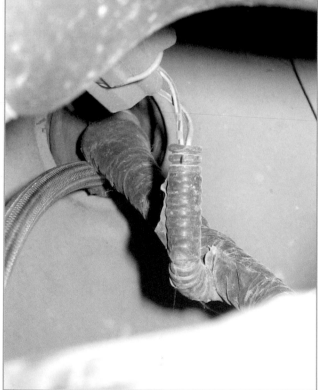

The line was wire tied along the tank. Another wire tie was used as it rounded a corner along a fuel line. As the line runs along the frame rail of the car, it is near the fuel and brake lines. Attach it to the existing mounts and lines about every 12 inches with a plastic wire tie. Don't leave too big of gap between wire ties, the line should not sag or it could catch or drag. Make sure that the line stays away from moving parts, sharp edges, and hot components, such as the exhausts. On the Honda Civic the exhaust runs down the passenger's side and the nitrous was on the driver's side. When you get to the firewall, run the nitrous line up the firewall making sure it will not get tangled in any of the linkage or steering components.

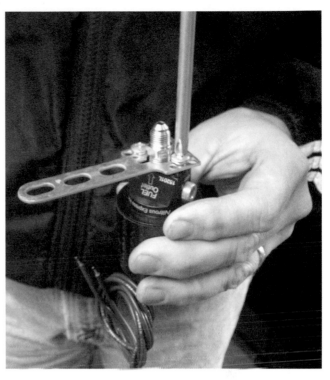

Left: The installation kit comes with brackets that hold the solenoids. All that needs to be done is to find a mounting location that will provide access to the lines and reach the nozzle. On the firewall were a couple of accessible bolts holding the cruise control unit. Two bolts and two solenoids—it was a perfect place. It was also close enough that the 12-inch lines from the solenoids to the nozzle would be long enough. Right: Install the solenoids in the brackets with the enclosed bolts. Note that anything to do with the nitrous is color-coded blue and anything dealing with the fuel is red—simple ways to make sure the right lines are going to the right places. Even the solenoids are color-coordinated.

After the solenoids are attached to the bracket, attach the bracket to the mount.

Install the nipples and lines to the solenoids. Make sure you use the red Teflon thread coating provided in the kit. DO NOT use just any Teflon tape. Again, red to red and blue to blue. There are two caps that screw into place on the purge openings. These will be used later when purging the system of air.

Attach the lines to the nozzle and then figure where the nozzle will be installed in the intake system. The instructions recommend somewhere around 6 inches from the intake, but then the instructions also go on to state that it really doesn't matter. The location I picked was based on the length of the lines, access to the nozzle, and access to the nozzle's mounting bracket that I needed to install in the intake. Mark the location with a marker.

Left: Remember when I mentioned that you would need to remove the intake again? Well, now's the time. After you marked the intake, remove it and place it securely on a bench or in a clamp and drill a hole for the nozzle's installation nut. The location is important because the nozzle nut will stick up through the intake and a lock nut will hold the assembly in the intake. The nozzle will then screw into the installation nut. *Right:* After drilling the hole, I used my Dremel with a small sanding drum to smooth all the edges and deburr the hole.

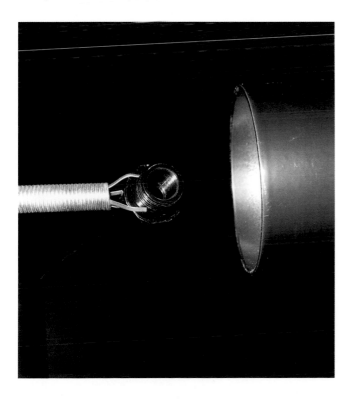

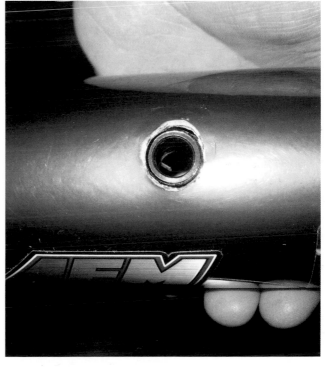

Using the flexible finger tool, I inserted the nozzle installation nut into the intake and placed it in the hole, threads to the outside.

*Left: Next, place the lock nut on the installation nut and tighten just finger-tight. The nozzle needs to be installed before the assembly is locked in place. **Right:** Place the nozzle in the installation nut until the threads touch. Thread the nozzle all the way into the installation nut.*

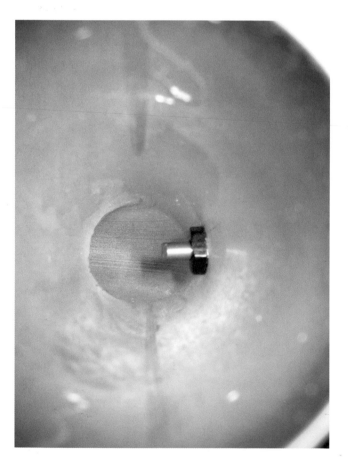

*Left: Looking down into the intake from the air filter end (straight end), make sure that the nozzle is aligned so that its opening is toward the curve of the intake and the throttle body. While holding the nozzle in that position, tighten the lock nut with an open-end wrench. **Right:** Just before you attach the lines, insert the jets into the nozzle. The NX system provides assorted nozzle sizes for the different horsepower settings. Start with the smallest size that is recommended in the manual. In our case we inserted an 18 in the fuel line and a 31 in the nitrous.*

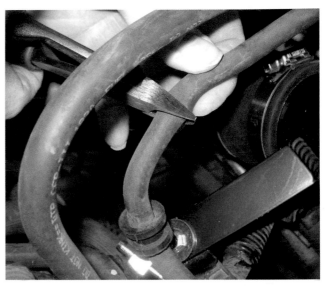

Left: Connect the lines from the solenoids to the nozzle. Make sure that you connect the correct line to the correct side of the nozzle. Right: Locate the fuel supply line. Typically these lines are pressurized so you need to make sure the fuel system is off and the pressure has been reduced. If you decide to cut the line anyway, have a fuel-proof container located under the line to collect the fuel as it drains from the line. It shouldn't be too big of a mess. Using a razor knife, or in my case a pair of diagonal cutters, clip the line in two.

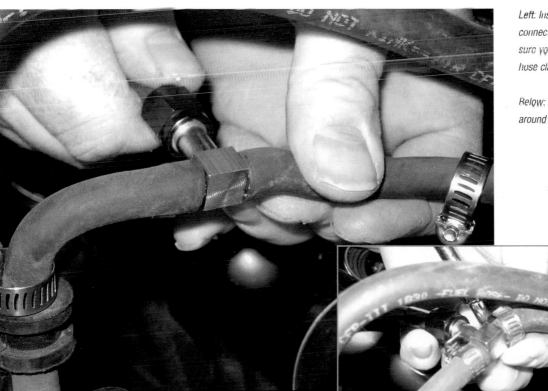

Left: Install the supplied T connector in the fuel line. Make sure you place the worm gear hose clamps on the lines first.

Below: Tighten the hose clamps around the T fitting.

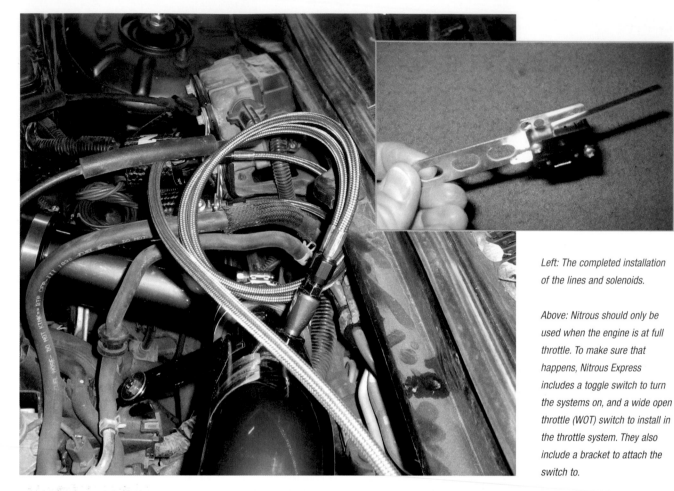

Left: The completed installation of the lines and solenoids.

Above: Nitrous should only be used when the engine is at full throttle. To make sure that happens, Nitrous Express includes a toggle switch to turn the systems on, and a wide open throttle (WOT) switch to install in the throttle system. They also include a bracket to attach the switch to.

Left: The bracket needed to be twisted 90 degrees. This might not be necessary on your installation.After the bracket is twisted, install the switch. The switch was going to be mounted on the backside of the throttle body and the trigger of the switch would be depressed by the throttle assembly. *Right:* To mount the WOT bracket in the correct area required making a support out of scrap metal found in the garage. I bent the scrap 90 degrees on one end to attach to a bolt on the firewall. Just past the WOT attachment point, the scrap was bent down about an inch and then straight out again. The scrap was shortened and bolted to a location near the throttle body.

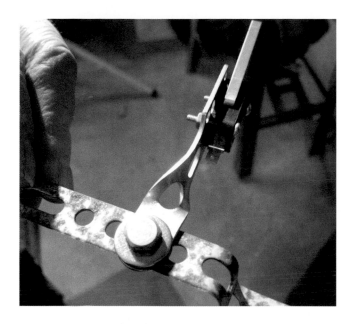

*Left: Attach the bracket and the switch to the new mount made from scrap metal. Your situation will probably be different. **Right:** The WOT switch in position; note where the trigger is pointing. When the accelerator pedal is depressed completely, the throttle assembly will depress the trigger on the switch, allowing the nitrous to be injected into the engine.*

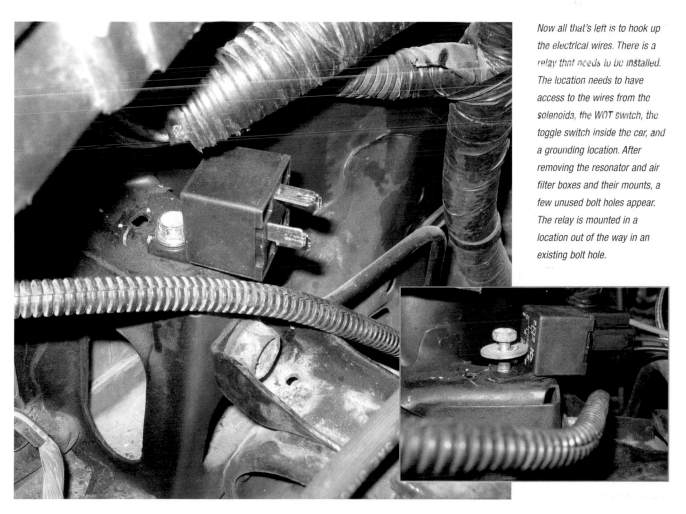

Now all that's left is to hook up the electrical wires. There is a relay that needs to be installed. The location needs to have access to the wires from the solenoids, the WOT switch, the toggle switch inside the car, and a grounding location. After removing the resonator and air filter boxes and their mounts, a few unused bolt holes appear. The relay is mounted in a location out of the way in an existing bolt hole.

Left: This air manifold is available at Left: Install the relay with the bolt removed from the mounting hole and tighten it securely in place. The relay will be connected to the wires from solenoids and the switches. Make sure you don't lose the instructions for the wiring!

Below: Connect two of the wires from the solenoids (we used the center wires, but it is a DC current so it doesn't matter which two) and crimp them along with the white wire from the relay into a ring terminal connector (supplied).

Left: Attach the wires and the ring terminal to the grounding bolt. Right: The red wire from the relay will be connected with a spade connector to the wide open switch, connected at the end terminal. The green wire from the relay will be connected to the remaining two wires on the solenoids. The black wire from the relay will connect to the ground or negative terminal of the battery.

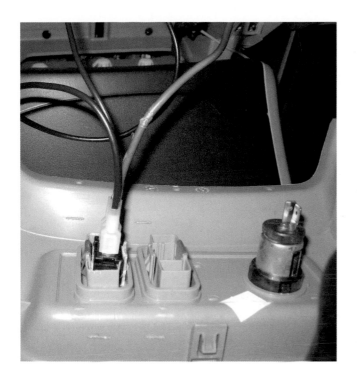 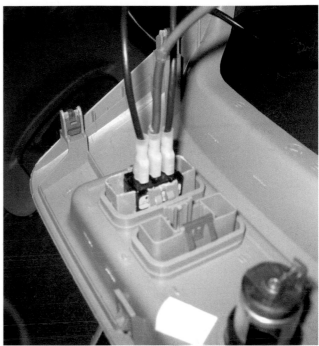

Left: Remove the accessory panel in the dash by just pulling it out. Disconnect the power plug. You can drill a hole in the panel to insert the toggle switch, or modify the accessory "plug" to hold the toggle switch. Since I was adding carbon dash panels I opted to modify the existing plug for the toggle switch. *Right:* Once the toggle switch is installed, one terminal needs to be attached to a ground and the other terminal needs to be attached to a switched power source. Run a wire from the center terminal on the toggle switch through an opening in the firewall and connect it to the side terminal of the WOT switch. After all the connections are complete, connect the battery, turn on the key (do not start the engine), and test the switches and see if the solenoids work. The solenoids should only work when the WOT switch is depressed and the toggle switch is turned on.

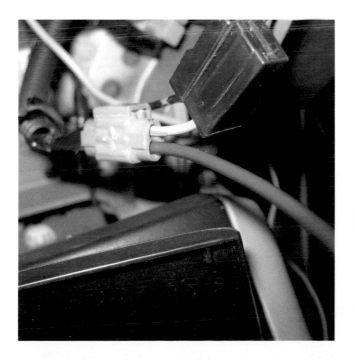 

Left: Connect the power terminal to a switched power source. The accessory power outlet is controlled by the key so I tapped in there with a splice connector.
Right: After all the connections are made to the toggle switch and it has been tested, snap the panel back in place.

145

Above: Make one last check of the connections and secure the wires out of the way with wire ties. *Below:* The lines were a little close to the hood so I wrapped them with foam insulation to make sure they didn't rub. I also put a small piece of insulation around the main nitrous line where it was touching the intake. I didn't want the new powder coat finish to get scratched.

CHAPTER 16
INSTALLING GAUGES

If you have nitrous, the engine runs harder and puts out more horsepower. That also means you need to keep a closer eye on what's going on under the hood. One way to do that is to add instruments and gauges. You should install a nitrous pressure gauge, fuel pressure gauge, oil temperature gauge, and a water temperature gauge. That covers the basics. Watch the pressures and the temperatures.

If that's more than the budget allows, look into fuel and nitrous pressure gauges. But watch the idiot lights closely if you leave out the temperature gauges. Usually by the time they come on, it's too late.

If you can't afford any gauges, don't worry, you can still run the nitrous, you just won't really know what's happening under the hood. Each run will be like a test run—who knows what kind of surprise you will get.

I used Auto Meter Competition Gauges. They offer all types of options and are very reasonably priced. Actually they have more options than I could comprehend. I finally asked Kris Carlson at Auto Meter Gauges to put together a budget package that would work for the modifications we were putting on the car. After Carlson was done, I had four gauges: oil pressure, water temperature, fuel pressure, and nitrous pressure. I also had a pillar mount that held two gauges and two separate carbon fiber mounts.

Remove the existing pillar trim—you could leave it in place but it needs to be modified slightly. At the base I drilled a 1-inch hole for the gauge wires to pass through.

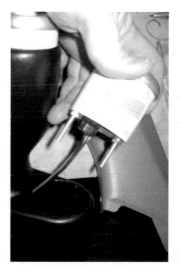

Above: The new pillar mount needs to be placed on the old mount and four 3/16-inch holes drilled in the corners. There are plastic push rivets that will be used to hold the pillar mount in place.

Left: Installing the gauges in the pillar mount is very simple. There are no retainer mounts; they are designed as a press-in fit.

Above: Each gauge has a wire loom that will run through the firewall to the sending unit and power source. Each gauge also has a light that will be connected to the dash lights. The dash light wires needed to be extended to reach under the dash. I used splice crimps and red and black wire the same length as the rest of the looms. I taped all the wires together at about 6-inch intervals to make it easier to work with and feed through the dash.

Right: I used a piece of 1/8-inch wire as a wire pull. I fed it up from under the dash and put a small loop in the end. I passed the wire looms through the 1-inch hole in the original pillar trim and connected the wire looms to the hook. As I pulled the wires through the dash, I worked the original trim and the new pillar mount back into place.

Above: In the 3/16-inch holes that were drilled insert the plastic push rivets to hold the pillar mount in place. Below: Connect the nitrous into the sending unit that is mounted in the adapter on the solenoid. The electronic sender plugs into the wire harness. Do the same with the fuel pressure gauge. Attach the sending unit to the adapter mounted on the solenoid and plug in the harness. Connect the wires to the power source and the ground.

Once the wires are pulled through the dash and coiled on the floor underneath, I put the original trim in place and pushed the new pillar mount over the top.

CHAPTER 17
INTERIOR MODIFICATIONS

Thinking that the interior of the Civic was kind of boring, I tried to come up with a simple way to jazz it up. After looking at many options—most of which cost way too much—I decided to install carbon fiber dash panels. These panels are available in all sorts of colors and patterns from Superior Dash. I opted for carbon fiber because I wanted that "racer" image. Plus, that goes with the aluminum floor mats, right? I decided on blue carbon fiber to accent the blue exterior and the boring brown interior.

Make sure you read the instructions thoroughly. You will need to have good lighting and the surfaces need to be clean.

Trial-fit the parts and decide on how you are going to install each piece to make sure they are positioned correctly. It sometimes helps to have another set of hands to hold the part away from the surface. Once it sticks it's stuck. The adhesive is very strong.

Because I did a trial fit for the parts, they fit very well in the end.

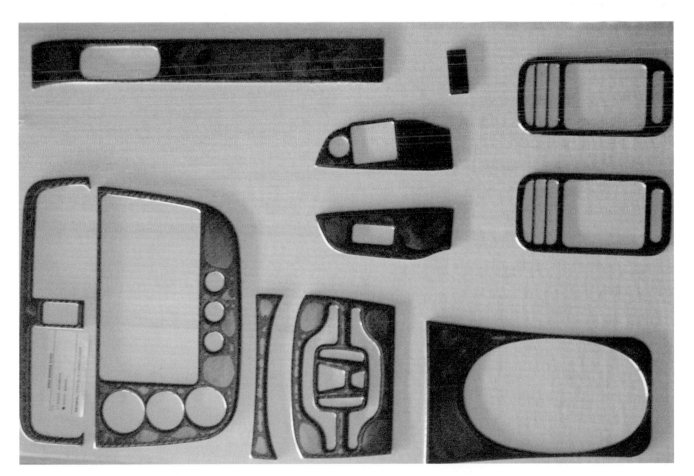

Superior Dash kits come complete and ready to install. They are vacuum-packed and look great. Clean the original surface with isopropyl alcohol and dry it.

Right: Using a hair dryer or a heat gun on low, warm the dash and the appliqué—don't overheat. Try to get it to about 100 degrees; this gives the parts a little more flexibility. If the dash and the appliqué are the same temperature, the parts will stay in shape better.

Below left: Carefully remove the plastic film from the adhesive. Place the carbon panel and press it firmly into place. Be careful—this stuff sticks. You might want to remove just half of the film until the panel is in place. Once it is pressed down, there is no getting it back up.

Left: Press the appliqué in place. Depending on the part, you may have to start at the bottom and work up. I found it better to fit around the switches and buttons first, then move outward. That's all there is to it. Repeat on the console, doors, and dash. *Right:* The completed dash and center console. Notice the "H" in the cup holder cover.

Above: Even the door gets the treatment.

Right: Superior includes an accent strip for the glove box.

INSTALLING FLOOR PANELS

Installing new floor panels was a pretty easy task. Performance Import Trends offers a diamond plate aluminum floorboard. I admit this is kind of a frivolous item to add to the car, but the old carpets had a few grease stains and this was easier than cleaning the carpets. Plus, it gives it a "racer" look.

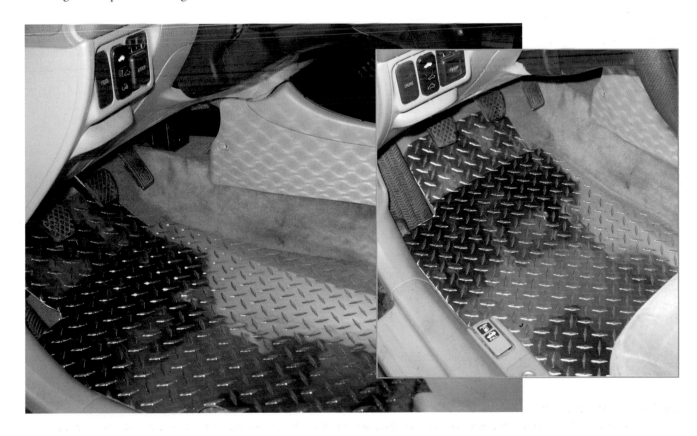

Installed floor boards.

CHAPTER 18
APPLYING GRAPHICS

Since we were not planning to paint the complete car, one way to offer personalization was a graphics package. There are hundreds of different graphics available. I wanted something that would accent the colors of the car, and also make a statement. I was looking through the Sharpline Graphics website and located a design in its Street Art section. The design looked kind of like a strike of lightning. It was called the "Re-volt." The design has blue, reddish, and silver edging.

I liked it but I left the final decision up to my daughter. Well it wasn't pink, which she wanted, but it would work. Kids; what do they know about graphics anyway?

I was surprised how big it was. When I unrolled the graphic, I thought it was bigger than the car, but it wasn't. It was just about the right length to go from the rear of the front wheel well to the back quarter panel. Exactly what I wanted.

Clean the sides of the vehicle with soap and water and a solvent of some sort. I used a cloth that had been dampened with isopropyl alcohol. Do not use paint thinner, acetone, etc. Makes sure the car is warm. Do not try to install the graphics if the temperature is too low, less than 65 degrees, or too hot, more than 80 degrees. Dry the vehicle with a lint-free cloth.

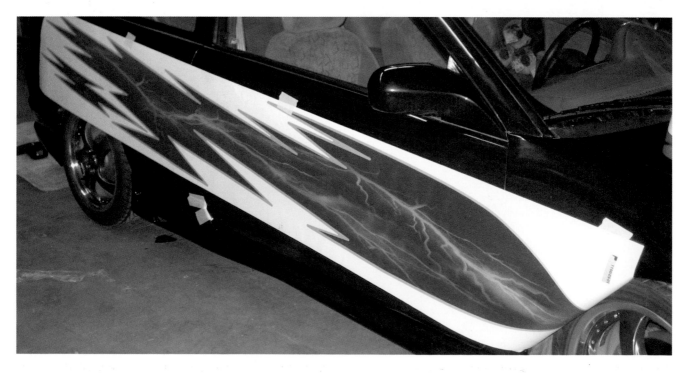

After the car is clean, position the graphic in the location you want and tape it in place with masking tape.

Left: If satisfied with the location, run a strip of masking tape through the center of the graphic as a "hinge" point. *Right:* Starting at the front, peel the graphics away from the paper backing and attach it or have someone hold it. You will only peel the graphic back to the "hinge" position.

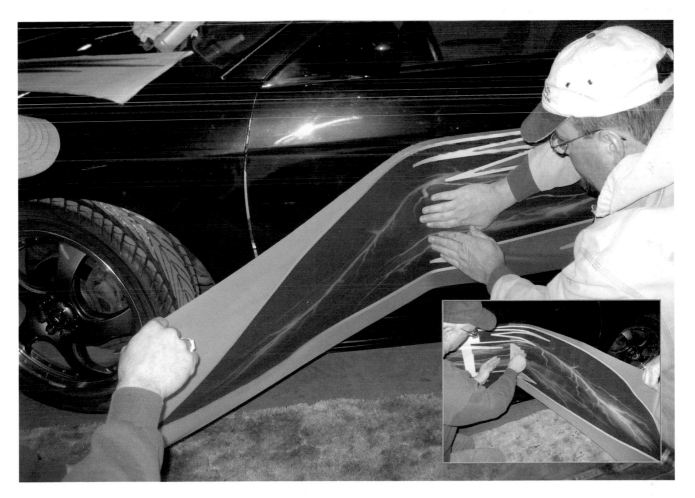

Slowly start pressing the graphic against the vehicle at the center of the graphic and, starting at the hinge line, work to the outer edges of the graphic. Use a plastic squeegee to work out the air bubble. Repeat the process from the hinge line to the other end of the graphic.

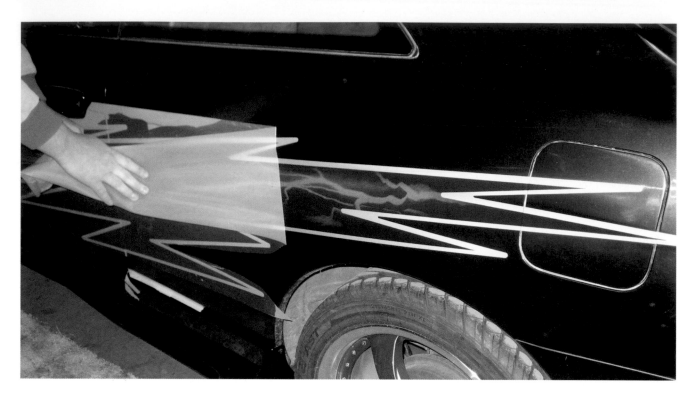

Remove the clear outer sheet, pulling it at a 180-degree angle from the vehicle.

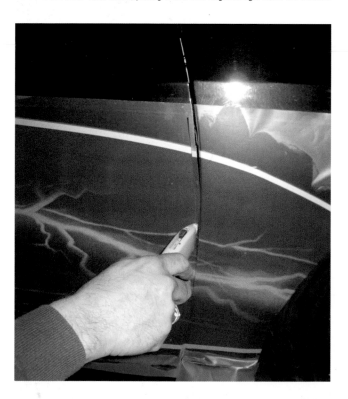

Left: Small air bubbles can be removed by poking tiny holes in the bubble with a razor knife and squeezing out the air. Use a razor knife to cut the graphics at all of the joints (door, fenders, gas cap, etc.). Sharpline recommends cutting the material at a 45-degree angle at both edges and removing the thin strip of excess material. If you try to fold the material over the edge it will not stick properly and the graphic will probably come loose. *Right:* We added a couple of leftover lightning bolts to the hood. As with the rest of the graphics, lay it down and tape in place using a hinge point.

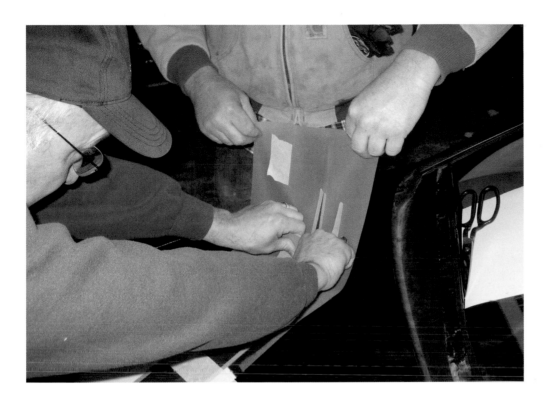

Remove half of the paper backing and squeegee the graphic to the hood. Repeat with the other half of the lightning bolt. Work all the air bubbles out.

All the graphics are in place.

CHAPTER 19
THE COMPLETED PROJECT

Finally, the car was done. With less than the cost of a standard car, we were able to put together a car with better performance, handling, and looks. I know you are all thinking, "this sounds good on paper, but how much did this thing really cost?"

Well, here is the final breakdown. There are a few odds and ends I haven't added in, assorted wires and tape, things I had in my shop. Of course this didn't count the new shed I added so I had more room; it's only the car parts. I didn't even add any new tools into the cost. Just the car and the modifications.

The breakdown:

2002 Honda Civic EX, 110,000 miles and with a salvage title	$4,800
New 17-inch tires and wheels	$975
Razzi ground effects	$1,100
PIT Cat Back Exhaust	$530
PIT Header	$340
PIT Carbon fiber wing I didn't use but still have	$175
Nitrous Express nitrous kit	$610
AEM short ram intake	$170
LSD Door kit	$1,990
ST Springs	$230
Superior Carbon Fiber Dash	$200
American Gauges	$610
Sharpline Re-Volt Graphics	$200
Custom paint for the ground effects parts	$1,100

Was it worth it? You bet. The car looks good and drives better.

TOOL AND SUPPLY CHECKLIST

Not all of the following are required but can help move the projects along.

3/8-inch ratchet

3/8-inch assorted sockets and drivers

3/8-inch extensions, assorted lengths

3/8-inch universal joint

3/8-inch spark plug socket (usually 5/8 or 13/16)

1/2-inch ratchet and sockets will work and might be helpful in a few situations

Acetone or paint thinner

Adjustable wrench

Air chisel

Air compressor

Air ratchet

Baking soda

Battery charger

Battery-post cleaning brush

Bench vise

Brush, wire for drill

Can opener, for filter

Clamps, assorted sizes and styles

Clean drain pan

Clean soft cloth

Combination wrench, assorted sizes metric and SAE (I like the ratcheting type)

Cordless drill

Cut-out tool and bits (for bumper)

Degreaser, spray

Diagonal cutters (wire cutters)

Dremel tool, cordless 8000 Lithium Ion Cordless Dremel tool bits (wire brush, grinding disk, sanding drum, cut-out kit and bits)

Extension cords

Fender cover or mechanics pad

Fire extinguisher

Fuel-proof drip pan

Gallon bucket

Hammer

Impact wrench (air, cordless or electric)

Isopropyl alcohol

Jack, floor style, 2-3 ton

Jack stands or blocks

Lug wrench

Magnet

Mechanics adjustable seat

Mechanics creeper

Mechanics mirror, telescoping 2x3

Metal can for soaking small parts

Paint gun

Paint, color-matched for Razzi ground effects parts

Penetrating oil (Liquid Wrench or similar)

Plastic dishes to put baking soda in, small

Pliers

Power buffer and pad (or cordless drill with buffing pad)

Protective battery terminal spray

Pry bar

Ramps, wheel

Razor knife

Rubber mallet

Sandpaper (80-, 180-, 320-, 400-, 600-, 800-,1,200-grit)

Sanding block

Screwdrivers, assorted

Sealer, silicone

Shop lights, trouble lights, light stands and flashlights

Silicone spray, CRC

Solvent, parts cleaning (paint thinner will work)

Solvent, acrylic friendly (Goo Gone)

Tape, electricians

Tape, duct

Tape, masking

Thread compound

WD-40

Wet/dry vacuum, Shop-Vac

Wire ties, assorted sizes.

Wire, lightweight for holding cables and parts

RESOURCES

Ankeny Auto Body
1501 SE Cortina Dr.
Ankeny, IA 50021
515-964-7291
www.ankenyautobody.com

Auto Meter Products, Inc.
413 W. Elm St.
Sycamore, IL 60178
Sales: 815-899-0800; Technical Service: 815-899-0801
www.autometer.com

Bosch Power Tools
1800 West Central Rd.
Mount Prospect, IL 60056
www.boschtools.com

Dremel
Robert Bosch Tool Corporation
1800 West Central Rd.
Mount Prospect, IL 60056
www.dremel.com

Elite Styling and Sound
109 SW 63rd St.
Des Moines, IA 50312
515-279-7800
www.elitestylingandsound.com

Klein Tools, Inc.
450 Bond St.
PO Box 1418
Lincolnshire, IL 60069-1418
800-553-4676
www.kleintools.com

Nitrous Express, Inc.
5411 Seymour Hwy.
Wichita Falls, TX 76310
940-767-7694
www.nitrousexpress.com

Performance Import Trends
PO Box 3090
Des Moines, IA 50316
866-639-8845
www.performance-trends.com

Razzi Ground Effects
1050 Branch Dr.
Alpharetta, GA 30004
800-235-6087
www.RAZZI.com

Shop-Vac
2323 Reach Rd.
PO Box 3307
Williamsport, PA 17701
570-326-0502
www.shopvac.com

Superior Dash
1960 S Segrave St.
Daytona Beach, FL 32119
800-741-3274
www.superiordash.com

The Tire Rack
7101 Vorden Pkwy.
South Bend, IN 46628
888-541-1777
www.tirerack.com

INDEX

Other titles of interest

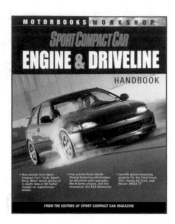

Sports Compact: Engines and Drivelines Handbook
#136305, 978-0-7603-1636-8

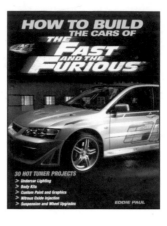

How To Build the Cars of The Fasst and the Furious
#138696, 978-0-7603-2077-8

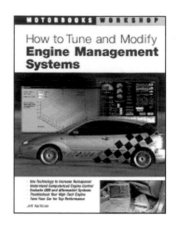

How to Tune and Modify Engine Management Systems
#136272, 978-0-7603-1582-8

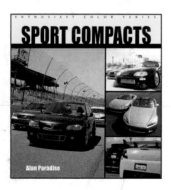

Sport Compacts
#135810, 978-0-7603-1496-8

Honda and Acura Performance Handbook
#137410, 978-0-7603-1780-8

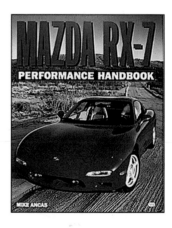

Mazda RX-7 Performance Handbook
#129797, 978-0-7603-0802-8

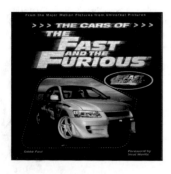

The Cars of The Fast and the Furious
#135815, 978-0-7603-1551-4

Custom Pickup Handbook
#139348, 978-0-7603-2180-5

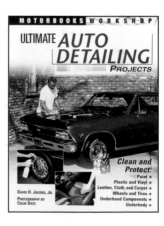

Ultimate Auto Detailing Projects
#135939, 978-0-7603-1448-7